WHAT PEOPLE ...

THE ESSENTIAL MES...

*Shaykh Fadhlalla Haeri's* The ... *invites the Western reader into a deep understanding of this important sacred text. As much misunderstood as the Qur'an is today, particularly in the popular media, so much more so does its wisdom and spiritual message offer insight on our present challenges. Major themes are the deeply ecological basis of sacred creation, the unity of understanding and including all of the world's religious ideals, and the simple message of justice and caring for those less fortunate than ourselves. Much of this has been overlooked or ignored by those who wish to extract a merely political message from a sacred book, similar to the way in which this has been done with the Bible, the Gita and other sacred treasures of humanity. Friendly on the reader,* The Essential Message of the Qur'an *offers a short commentary on each of the Qur'an's major themes, linked to a selection of passages illustrating it. As such, it is a wonderful introduction for any person who wonders how to approach the living book and experience the blessing and wisdom experienced by millions around the world today.*
**Dr. Neil Douglas-Klotz,** author of *The Sufi Book of Life* and others

*A treasure trove for every person eager to find balance, hope and, yes, light in the shadows of this world. It is a gift for every reader who is not content with the standard or one-dimensional view of Islam as another world religion, and the Qur'an as a closed book with no connection or message for those outside the orb of Arabia or Islam. Its message is as wise as it is welcome.*
**Dr. Bruce B Lawrence,** Duke University

*Shaykh Fadhlalla Haeri has written one of the most accessible, readable and informative introductions to the Qur'an.* The Essential Message of the Qur'an *carries the imprint of a person who has spent a lifetime* immersed in the study of the Qur'an, and can rightly be considered as one of its authoritative modern interpreters. The book provides all the necessary keys to the appropriate reading of the Qur'an and clearly demonstrates the spiritual significance of the sacred text and how it has inspired countless millions across the ages.

I can think of no better way to understand the meaning of the Qur'an than to begin with this valuable introduction.

**Ali A. Allawi,** Author of *The Crisis of Islamic Civilization* and *Winning the War, Losing the Peace*

# The Essential Message of the Qur'an

# The Essential Message of the Qur'an

Shaykh Fadhlalla Haeri

BOOKS

Winchester, UK
Washington, USA

First published by O-Books, 2011
O-Books is an imprint of John Hunt Publishing Ltd., Laurel House, Station Approach,
Alresford, Hants, SO24 9JH, UK
office1@o-books.net
www.o-books.com

For distributor details and how to order please visit the 'Ordering' section on our website.

Text copyright: Shaykh Fadhlalla Haeri 2010

ISBN: 978 1 84694 701 8

All rights reserved. Except for brief quotations in critical articles or reviews, no part of this book may be reproduced in any manner without prior written permission from the publishers.

The rights of Shaykh Fadhlalla Haeri as author have been asserted in accordance with the Copyright, Designs and Patents Act 1988.

A CIP catalogue record for this book is available from the British Library.

Design: Lee Nash

Printed in the UK by CPI Antony Rowe
Printed in the USA by Offset Paperback Mfrs, Inc

We operate a distinctive and ethical publishing philosophy in all areas of our business, from our global network of authors to production and worldwide distribution.

# CONTENTS

| | |
|---|---|
| Prologue | 1 |
| Foreword | 5 |
| Chapter 1: Qur'an and Revelation | 14 |
| Chapter 2: God's Light | 32 |
| Chapter 3: Creation | 54 |
| Chapter 4: Adam and Human Nature | 72 |
| Chapter 5: Earthly Life and the Hereafter | 92 |
| Chapter 6: Prophets of Islam | 116 |
| Chapter 7: Salvation and Enlightenment | 134 |
| Qur'anic References | 151 |

# Prologue

In Karbala, my childhood Qur'an was calligraphed and block printed on 30 large glossy sheets, produced around 1920 in Lucknow, India. My father's Qur'an was presented to him in the year it was produced, and had four different commentaries in the margin. Printed Qur'ans were scarce at the time, often only available in chapters for memorisation. Many Iraqi families had their own handwritten or block printed Qur'ans – and it was only from the 1930s that modern printed versions became available. The Muslim public had put up considerable resistance to the printing of the Qur'an due to fear of desecration, disrespect or contamination by the ink, which may have contained unclean substances such as alcohol. Early printing presses in Istanbul and Cairo were boycotted by Muslims for many decades during the 19th century due to these concerns.

In the cities of the newly formed state of Iraq during the late 1920s, government schools slowly began to replace the traditional Qur'an *madrassahs*. These were outdated and restricted to teaching the Qur'an by rote to children often by tutors with limited education, who were harsh towards youngsters. The secular western style education was fairly prevalent throughout the country during my childhood and learning Qur'an by heart was soon a practice of the past for young Iraqis. Local habits and customs – including the culture of Qur'anic Arabic and poetry recitation – were fast changing. Magazines and novels were imported from Egypt, Lebanon and the West as a prelude to radio and television distractions.

Several times a year, Karbala was visited by Bedouin camel caravans of various sizes to trade their goods and to visit the shrine of the martyred Imam Hussein and his brother, Abbas. As a child, I was fascinated by the intricate and unusual linguistic relationship between the members of the visiting nomadic tribe. The extent of the freedom of women and children were awarded was markedly different from us city folk. I would often tease Baba Mahmoud, my guardian, by playfully hiding behind camels or tents. The child in me was fascinated by the immense differences between the ancient, dynamic ways of these free-spirited Bedouins and the sedentary habits of the conservative, settled urbanised people. The ancient Semitic language spoken by these Bedouins hadn't changed much over the centuries, and it differed drastically from the language and culture of us civilised folk. The gulf between the oral culture and the restrictive, literate ways left a lasting impression in my young mind.

Islam's key tenets lie in considering God as central to everything in existence and that this world and life on earth is only a preparation to the next. Personal earthly life will end with the death of the body, whereas the soul's life continues into the realm of the hereafter. All human beings are the offspring of Adam, as related in the Qur'an, and are equal in the eye of God although on earth there are obvious differences in power, wealth, knowledge, and so on. The ancient tribal democracy acknowledged outer hierarchy and authority but emphasised equality in the eye of God, openness in self-expression and freedom.

The difference between the ancient Arabs and today's Arabic-speaking people can clearly be witnessed in the modern Arabic usage as compared to Qur'anic Arabic. The Arabic in the Qur'an is considerably different to the modern versions used by ordinary folks. The Arabic language is rooted in the ancient Semitic tongue, which had remained unchanged for at least 2000 years. Classical scholars of the Qur'an often blame city folks for the corruption of the original Arabic. It is said that some of the Qur'an's language relate to camels, nomadic culture and its special worldview. Therefore, in order to truly understand the full depth of the meanings of the Qur'an, we need to visualise the way of life and mindset of people at that time. This is a major reason why the Qur'an cannot be adequately translated. In addition to the linguistic and cultural barriers related to the full appreciation of the Qur'an, the reader needs to reflect and resonate with its transformative energy. For the door of insights and lights to open upon the inner ear and heart, the approach to the Qur'an must be based on humility, faith and trust in God's ever-present mercy and grace. When opening up to the multidimensionality of the Qur'an, we need to leave behind personal credentials, knowledge and other aspects of identity or separation from Allah's cosmic light.

Many years after leaving Karbala, when I began to share the beauty and perfection of the Qur'an with non-Arabs, I realised how impossible it is to simply translate it into another language. The Qur'an is understood by one's total immersion in the Qur'an. My experience of trying to make the message of the Qur'an accessible to non-Arabs encouraged me to write this book. It is based on personal interpretations of key topics and issues drawn from the Qur'an's numerous references to them.

# Foreword

This brief book is written for anyone interested to know the basic message and purpose of the Qur'an, and its historical, cultural and religious framework. It highlights the important issues and topics of the Qur'an for the serious Muslim as well as others interested in religion, spirituality or the search for meaning.

Muslims consider the Qur'an as the most essential and revered reference for all aspects of life of mankind. It is considered to be the last complete Divine Revelation and is totally devoid of any human interference. It reveals primary patterns and designs that are the essence of the entire universe and creation therein, all of which is held by God's unifying power and will – the sacred Oneness, which is not limited by space or time.

The Qur'an and the Prophet's conduct are the two main foundations of the path of Islam, which are used as guidelines regarding existential matters such as human relationships, interaction with the environment and other creations, and formal and transformative worship. The Qur'an describes the whole universe as being in total submission to God, following the perfect patterns of dualities and the cycles of limits and deaths in different ways. From the absolute Oneness emanates countless dualities and pluralities all interacting according to their innate ability or power. This is the soul of sentient creatures, with Adam's soul being the closest in the knowledge of God's light and spirit.

The Qur'an shows through symbols, metaphors and actual historical events the ideal behaviour man needs to follow in order to be fulfilled and complete. It directs us how to transcend purely material concerns and deal with egotistic distractions so that we can arrive at the state of enlightenment and fulfilment at heart.

Historically, the Qur'an was revealed to the Prophet Mohammed during the year 610 (Christian era) whilst he was meditating in the cave of Hira, on the mount of light, during the month of Ramadan. It was the Prophet's habit every year to spend much time in seclusion and reflection. On this year, which was his fortieth, the angel Jibra'il appeared to him during the Night of Power (during the last 10 days of the month of Ramadan) and commanded him to read - *Iqra*, from which one of the names the Qur'an is derived.

This event was of a major significance to the life of the Prophet. It marked the revival of Islam (the surrender to God) and the culmination of a striving of the long line of Abrahamic cultures and traditions. Although the Qur'an in its entirety descended upon the heart of the Prophet like lighting, its actual manifestation through Jibra'il took twenty-three years connecting worldly situations with the message and its multifaceted meanings.

The Qur'an describes itself by numerous nouns and names, many of which are used interchangeably by Muslims. One of its names is Al-Furqan, the discrimination (between true and false). Other names include Al-Mushaf (collection of pages), Al-Dhikr (remembrance) and many others. Its language and style follows its own unique rules and is a combination of poetic and prose styles. It is unlike any other scripture in that it was wholly revealed to one human being who lived and practised its message fully throughout his life. Its patterns, signs and injunctions have been reverently studied and followed by Muslims in every culture throughout the ages. The stories and parables in the Qur'an may relate to actual historical events but are also true and useful for all times and for all humankind.

The Qur'an is divided into 114 chapters, each is called a *surah* composed of several short or long verses, which vary widely in number called *ayahs* (signs). The Qur'an begins with the longest *surahs*, ends with the shorter ones and is divided into 30 almost equal proportions called *Juz*, for the convenience of reading one portion a day to complete it within a month. The *surahs* revealed at Mecca for 10 years before the Prophet's migration to Medina are called Meccan surahs and amounts to 86. These are generally short, powerful and passionate in their call of mankind to heed God's unique sovereignty and hold over the whole universe.

Allah's cosmic light is the Truth, which brings about life on earth and the hereafter. The Prophet and books that came after Abraham confirm the path of submission – Islam and transformation through faith in God, selfless actions and sincere worship. The Meccan ayahs reveal transcendental truth and describe the relationship of the transient earthly experience as the human duty to realise the purpose of life and its sacred gift. Relativeness of time and space in creation is shown to be insignificant in relation to God's eternal supreme light.

The revelations after the migration to Medina, in the year 622, are called Medina ayahs. This year is also the beginning of the Islamic lunar calendar. The Medina chapters and verses cover many aspects of regulatory considerations, including relationships between people and laws to govern the affairs of the nascent community, which helped to define its cultural boundaries and proper conduct. Some verses (and chapters) may have been revealed more than once (in Mecca or Medina) and have been the subject of much scholastic debate among Muslim scholars. Although the order of revelations follow from Mecca to Medina, there are some Meccan verses placed in Medina surahs, probably by the Prophet himself.

During the time of the Prophet, most of those close to him tried to memorise what was revealed to him. The pre-literate Arabs, renowned for their oral tradition, had sharp memories and easy retention. Early recordings of the Qur'an were also undertaken using pieces of papyrus, flat stones, animal shoulder blades, leather and skins, wooden boards, silk cloth and other materials. Many of the verses descended in a specific place and time relating to particular circumstances. Some early verses and injunctions were subsequently abrogated because they were limited and applicable only to their own time. As circumstances changed, these earlier injunctions were changed accordingly and superseded the previous ones.

Soon after the death of the Prophet, in 632 AD, the natural differences and inconsistencies in narration and in the copying down of the Qur'an began to appear. The writers' and recitors' backgrounds, personal opinions and vocal preference were obvious causes for differences. The original ancient Arabic script (called Kufi) was too basic and could only be read properly if instructed and trained by a teacher. Diacritical marks appeared many centuries later. By the time of the third caliph, Othman, it was quite obvious that there was an urgency to ensure authenticity and uniformity in the scripts that were copied and recited.

At this time, Islam was expanding fast and new people of different cultures and languages were embracing Islam. During Othman's time the original copies, especially those kept by order of the first caliph were collected and from these, five copies were calligraphed in Kufi script. These were sent to Damascus, Kufa, Basra, Yemen, Bahrain and two were kept in Mecca and Medina. Other manuscripts, which were in circulation from before, were destroyed. It is therefore correct to say that the Qur'an in our hand today is totally authentic and original with insignificant variations, if at all.

During the time of the Prophet only a few of the chapters were clearly titled; most of the others were named after a prominent incident, a person or a topic that is in the surah. After a few centuries most of the titles become traditionally accepted with some variations as we have them today. It was not until 200 years or so after the death of the Prophet that the diacritic marks began to appear – initially as black and red dots but within a century or so later much clearer versions appeared ending with a detailed marking as we have today.

The Qur'an contains moral stories such as those of the Prophet Abraham, and the sacrifice of his son, the teachings of the Prophet Moses by the mysterious Khidr and how Moses was brought up in the palace of the Pharaoh, his future enemy. There are also numerous descriptions of what happened to ancient peoples who transgressed, such as the Prophet Noah and the famous flood, and the Arabic people of Aa'd and Thamud. Other miraculous events show how worldly measures are relative and can occasionally be suspended by unforeseen forces or events. The immaculate conception of Mary, the People of the Cave, the Prophet Jonah and the whale, the drowning of the Pharaoh and his people are examples of such events.

Many of the stories are similar to those in the Bible, with some differences such as the crucifixion of Jesus and other events. There are, however, differences with what appears in the Hebrew and Christian scriptures. For example, some stories are particular to the Arab people and thus are not referred to in Judaeo-Christian teachings, such as the encounter of Moses and Khidr. The Qur'an is a single and integrated revelation and thus, it differs from the Bible, which is a collection of writings and inspirations relayed and not directly revealed. In Islam, the Prophet's teachings and utterances (called Hadith) are more like the Gospels.

The Qur'an describes the human condition, the path to salvation and happiness on earth as well as in the hereafter. As such, it links the unseen sacred state with that which is earthly and understandable by human beings. In this respect, the Judaeo-Christian believers were given special respect and named as the People of the Book, implying they had a belief in God and the hereafter and were followers of a real prophet. The western-trained mind, which is conditioned to be specific and definitive finds much difficulty with the Qur'anic language and its power of transmission, which appear to the non-Arab as deliberately vague. God is referred to, in the Qur'an, as I or We or Am, etc. This clearly indicates that God is not a person. The apparent lack of linguistic clarity highlights the more important issue: God is a being beyond human comprehension. God is the only Truth and Reality; all else is an apparent overflow from His Grace.

The few reliable and respected recitors during the time of the Prophet passed on the mantle to the next generation, who produced several famous third-generation authorities on proper recitation and accurate rendering. They came to be regarded as the forefathers of the historical, classical seven recitations. Only two of these famous seven ways had remained in circulation today. One is called *Hafs*, recited in majority of Muslim countries, and the other is called *Warsh*, recited predominantly in Morocco and other parts of North Africa. Both recitations are named after the well-known recitors of those names. These were two of seven famous and traditionally acknowledged recitors, who were prominent in different cities of the Muslim world.

Recitation and memorisation of the Qur'an had become the religious golden thread connecting all Muslim people up until our present day. Even if the reciter does not understand the meaning of what is read, he or she is awarded special status by Muslims. The sound of the Qur'an has a magical attraction and resonance to the human heart, irrespective of the scholarship of the producer of the sounds.

## Foreword

The Qur'an's language is unique as it connects worldly reason and discernment with higher consciousness and the spiritual domain. Therefore, it is not possible to translate it without a great deal of interpretations and explanations, thereby loosing much of the impact of its majestic beauty. For an Arabic speaking person, the roots of most words (often three letters) carry with them numerous vocal branches, which interrelate and resonate together. Therefore, the Qur'an's sounds are transformative and touch the listener's heart and deep essence.

The Arabic language is one of the ancient oral mediums of connecting discernible aspects of life with the unseen, whereas most modern languages have evolved to classify and differentiate all aspects of the tangible world. Many of the ancient Semitic or Aramaic terms meant the opposite at the same time whereas this apparent contradiction is rare in Indo-European languages. The language of the Qur'an deals with reason and human sensibility but relates them to transcendental realities and archetypes so a non-Arab scholar, who may be fluent in the Arabic language may still find many of the Qur'anic messages inconsistent and even contradictory. The word 'atrab' implying 'to be like dust', for example, could mean a person who is so poor that he is common like dust. The same term, pronounced in the same way, could also indicate a person so wealthy that gold is like dust to him.

Traditionally, the translation of the Qur'an into other languages was frowned upon by formal scholars and doctors of Islam. The Qur'an remained un-translated until 1153 when a Latin edition appeared. Then in 1649, an English version (from French) was produced by Alexander Ross. This was followed in 1734 by George Sales, then a translation by J.M. Rodwell in 1861 and by E.M. Palmer in 1880. Even if some of these translations were not deliberately biased, they were difficult to follow and understand.

It was not until 1930 that Mohammed Marmaduke Pickthall produced his scholarly and sincere translation in Hyderabad using old language.

In 1934, Abdullah Yusuf Ali produced a translation containing many footnotes and explanations. In 1955, Arthur J. Arberry produced his translation followed in 1956 by N.J. Dawood. From thereon, numerous publishing houses, university presses and Muslim states began to produce their own versions. By the end of the 20$^{th}$ century, there were probably no less than 400 translations in different languages, with well over 100 in English alone.

Today, numerous other Qur'an commentaries and discourses continue to be produced in different languages for different purposes and audiences by academic and religious institutes. Interest in the language and grammar had been very common. Sufi or Gnostic commentaries have also occurred from classical times up to the present day. Naturally, there are considerable variations in the quality and depth of scholarship and research. The demand created by the thirst for Qur'anic knowledge is clearly on the increase throughout the world.

This book briefly tries to highlight some of the important topics mentioned in the Qur'an in a modern way so that it can benefit people from different cultures and backgrounds. Religious and Arabic terms have been deliberately avoided as the emphasis had been on the meanings of the messages. Also, a section on Qur'anic references has been provided listing the verses from which these essays have been synthesised. My emphasis in this book has been towards the inner meanings and transformative potential of the Qur'an rather than formal prescriptive aspects of it. I deliberately chose brevity and simplicity to highlight the connection between humanity and divinity, the seen and the unseen. The Qur'an's main emphasis is to highlight to humankind the understanding and knowledge of the sacred presence within the whole universe. The ultimate foundation of Islam is the declaration that there is no God except the One and only God and that the Prophet Muhammad is his messenger. Islam – submission to Truth – is not a new religion but the only reliable path trod upon by all the real Prophets and enlightened beings of the past and present.

## Chapter 1

## Qur'an and Revelation

Introduction
1.1  The Book of Signs and Metaphors
1.2  The Book of Guidance and Truth
1.3  The Book of Discrimination and Wisdom
1.4  A Universal Book
1.5  The Descent of the Qur'an
1.6  Approach to the Qur'an
1.7  Other Prophetic Messages
1.8  Necessity of Faith
1.9  The Real and Other Realities
1.10  Submission to Truth
1.11  Natural Illusions
1.12  Ever-Present Perfection
1.13  The Qur'an Reveals Itself

# 1

# Qur'an and Revelation

**Introduction**

The Qur'an is considered by Muslims as the culmination of the revelations that began with Abraham and expanded with Judaic and Christian texts and practices. The Prophet Muhammad is the seal of Prophets.

The Qur'an was revealed to the Prophet Muhammad in a most unique manner. The entire Qur'an and its light descended upon the Prophet on the 'Night of Power' (*Laylat al-Qadr*) when he was 40 years old, while the actual words and verses (*ayat*), in human language, were gradually revealed over the following 23 years of his life. This process allowed the messages, teachings and spiritual wisdom to be related in practical ways, integrated in everyday life and applied.

The Prophet's close companions and a few relatives narrated and recorded the specific circumstances surrounding the revelation of many of the verses, thus enabling a contextual understanding of the revelation. The chapters that were revealed in Mecca generally address all of mankind and their relation to God, while the Medinan chapters relate to correct personal and social conduct, worship and other social, political and legal issues. Many verses were revealed in relation to actual events or situations, thus providing relevant guidance and direction.

Many of the Prophet's close companions memorised and recorded parts of the Qur'an during his lifetime, but the rapid spread of Islam necessitated the standardisation of the original text. Othman, the third Caliph, undertook the task, using the Qurayshi dialect. The Othmani Qur'an was arranged mostly according to the length of the chapters and not according to chronology of revelation. This standard version was distributed to the main centres within the Muslim world and older variations were discarded or destroyed. A few years later, Caliph 'Ali Ibn Abi Talib established the codification of the rules of Arabic grammar and orthography. Since then, numerous Islamic scholars have excelled in diverse aspects of studies related to the Qur'an, from differing linguistic, historical, social and religious angles.

Qur'anic science covers its inimitability, exegesis or commentary, the historical context in which the verse was revealed, grammar, eloquence and traditional pronunciations and methods of reading. The Qur'an has also been referred to as the Book, the Light, the Balance, the Discrimination, the Guidance, and the Remembrance, amongst others. The Qur'an's power is due to its consistency regarding the truth that all of creation is held by God's unique cosmic will and Oneness; and its description of the patterns of creation, and the appropriate code of conduct by employing parables, historical stories and wise guidelines for personal and social wellbeing. The special language of the Qur'an bridges the gap between the unseen realm and the world of physical entities, logic and reason. It connects humanity with its essence of Divine Reality.

There are many levels of understanding the meanings of the Qur'an, from the common outer meanings to the deeper or subtler insights and lights with layers of subtle nuances of knowledge. Most verses (especially the Meccan *ayat*) have several such facets. The outer includes the recitation, the linguistic and cultural context, grammar, semantics, and historical understanding and references that are essential for proper comprehension. Numerous verses can only be fully understood by referring to other verses that highlight and clarify the intended meanings or injunctions.

The Qur'an contains the blueprint for the perfect manner of transaction with oneself, with society and the Creator. The Qur'an is like a universal Divine mirror that reflects whatever there is in the universe in a manner that can be understood and followed by any human being who seeks transformation and awakening to the everlasting source and essence that lies within the human heart. Much depends upon one's intention, faith and courteous approach to the sacred text. Indeed, wherever one looks there are signs of the Creator. We can only see due to His grace and generosity.

## 1.1 The Book of Signs and Metaphors

The Qur'an reveals patterns and maps of the universe, creation and the relationship to God of all that is known and unknown; it shines the truth upon what is in heaven and on earth; it connects the physical and material with unseen energies and realities; it draws analogies, similitudes and metaphors to patterns of connections based on the One field that pulsates throughout the universe; and it shows that human reason and logic are essential starting points that lead to subtler understandings, insights and higher consciousness.

The Qur'an affirms that all of creation glorifies Allah in subtle or obvious ways, consciously or otherwise, and clearly shows that there is meaning to all forms and events by referring to numerous created forms — from the smallest insects like bees and spiders to birds and other animals — and also elaborates upon key substances that are necessary for life, such as water, fire, earth and air. So, for instance, it highlights the flimsiness of the spider's web as a metaphor for the fragility of human life on earth. It narrates the lives and lessons of numerous people in history and the advent of prophets and messengers.

The Qur'an weaves a tapestry that shows us how the seen and the unseen connect and relate, and how, from God's eternal boundlessness, the universe and all of creation have emanated. It describes the human soul as earthly, but of sacred origin — the breath of God. Everything in existence is a sign of the ever-present Creator and His perfect, interactive design. All of these revelations show the faithful seeker a clear path towards the ever-present Divine light, which is the origin and destiny of the universe and all that exists within it. The Qur'an warns against heedlessness of the purpose of life and brings the good news of paradise — both here and the hereafter.

## 1.2 The Book of Guidance and Truth

Physical, worldly reality and appearances veil that which is the intrinsic nature or essence of existence and creation. Every form has a meaning and contains the essence — the spirit — that emanates from Allah. Thus, our earthly world is indicative of the subtler realm that becomes evident in the hereafter.

All human experiences relate to multiple strands of dualities and pluralities that connect causes and effects, and emanate from and ultimately return to God. Outer wisdom and understanding is part of evolvement, which may lead to insight and transformation that will have a lasting effect if it is internalised and assimilated.

The Qur'an is like a manual that explains the intricate connectedness of all forms and their energy fields — the highest of which is God consciousness. The human mind, heart and soul are instruments that can guide one out of earthly darkness to light. Numerous unseen powers, such as angels, also serve to guide us to a better destiny.

The spiritual seeker needs the guidance, teachings and examples of prophets and men of wisdom and knowledge as much as a child needs parental guidance for their personal and collective progress and wellbeing.

The Prophet and the Divine Revelations offer the ultimate, perfect guidance on earth — providing hope and contentment for people of faith who trust in God's infinite mercy.

With the correct intention and humbleness, whoever approaches the Qur'an will derive some benefit and will be exposed to higher horizons of consciousness and insights. Truth prevails within the entire universe and everything that exists carries a seed of that Truth.

## 1.3 The Book of Discrimination and Wisdom

The Qur'an reveals the intricate connections of the fabric of creation and the levels of causality. Every event or experience presents a challenge, from which we may grow in personal or spiritual wisdom.

Everything that we consider to be good is accompanied by the seed of that which we might judge as bad. Absolute goodness only belongs to God, as do all virtues and reliable qualities.

Clear reason, discrimination and justice are essential foundations for righteous actions, which may lead to openings of insights and spiritual wisdom beyond dualities and the interplay of light and shadows.

Humans can exercise justice by engaging in outer good deeds and reducing conflict and disruption. The path of wisdom implies the least distractions from the higher purpose of self-awareness and accountability. Thus, one might ideally reflect upon God's will and the perfection of the essence, meaning and purpose of life on earth.

Life on earth is like an intermediate state, between the state of pre-identity (before birth), and the return to non-identity (after death), where all of creation evolves towards higher consciousness. The Qur'an reminds human beings that the purpose in life is to remember their Creator and to awaken to His presence and governance on earth.

The Qur'an warns against denial or negligence in interacting with the physical world and urges people to do their best for all of creation with generosity and compassion. Our earthly life is a prelude to the next, subtler realm of the hereafter. Therefore living a balanced and wholesome life will lead to earthly as well as heavenly wisdom.

## 1.4 A Universal Book

The Qur'an not only encompasses all that concerns human life on earth, personally and collectively, but also universal issues. Its message bestows mercy and grace upon whomsoever absorbs it and lives accordingly.

Small issues are addressed alongside major ones. Everyday topics are connected to subtle, unseen roots, and put in proper perspective through the use of parables and the narration of historical events that highlight the human need to strive towards higher wisdom and judgment and the establishment of justice. It shows us that the treachery of the lower self (ego) is the inner *shaytan* (Satan) and how our self-justification and hypocrisy consistently lead to destructive outcomes.

God is incomparable beyond measure and the Qur'an reminds us to refer our earthly, discernable and measurable situations to that which is ever True and Real, yet unseen. The universe is like a womb woven by space and time, containing countless interacting entities, each bounded by birth and death, and restricted by other limitations. Discernment and discrimination come about whenever reason and causality take place within the confines of space and time, which in itself is a transient reality that floats in infinite timelessness. Humanity's earthly perch is an aspect of the universal realities.

The Qur'an emphasises the basic patterns that govern earthly realities and connect them to their heavenly root, to which all return. It illustrates how relative time and space are so that we may see our earthly concerns in the proper perspective through the remembrance of eternity. Through God consciousness, all other misunderstandings stabilise appropriately.

Heavenly stars and galaxies are described as being held together by Allah's will, up to an appointed time, after which they will disintegrate and return to the original singularity and nothingness.

## 1.5 The Descent of the Qur'an

The Qur'an in its entirety descended during the 'Night of Power' (*Laylat al-Qadr*) upon the Prophet's heart when his consciousness resonated with the Supreme consciousness. The Divine message of the Qur'an then began to unfold over many years as situations inspired the Prophet to speak out at the appropriate time and occasion. The verses of the Qur'an were thus revealed in the right context to illustrate the relevance of the sacred truth to human life and the challenges that people face under different circumstances. Gradually, the revelations began to weave a tapestry that showed the basic patterns that govern creation and the role and purpose of human beings on earth: to perfect worship of Allah.

Most of the revelations in Mecca relate to Allah as omniscient and omnipresent, the supreme actor, instigator and governor of whatever is contained in the heavens and earth. This powerful light of Divine unity dispels all notions of humans' experiential duality, separation and conflict. Supreme reality is the essence of all other realities, which derive their existence from it and seek it, knowingly or not.

In Medina, however, where a nascent community of Muslims began to emerge, it became necessary to have basic rules and regulations for conduct and transaction. Thus, we see that the mercy and justice applied and experienced on earth is a prelude to the perfect mercy and justice in the hereafter. Appropriate injunctions were revealed as problems arose in different times and places. Chapters and verses continued to descend for nearly 23 years to guide and reform the community of faithful followers of the Qur'an and the Prophet Muhammad, who memorised and recorded the specific reasons for their descent, as well as certain abrogations, many of which were simply a completion, addition or clarification of previous injunctions.

## 1.6 Approach to the Qur'an

In order to understand the Qur'an, it is a prerequisite to have the knowledge and capacity to grasp its multifaceted language. Its Arabic is unique and does not compare to any other tongue. The humble approach of the seeker, coupled with faith and trust in God, are necessary preconditions for absorption of the message and ultimately for personal transformation.

As the Qur'an relates the seen to the unseen worlds, both the head and heart need to be present. It is essential that one starts with humility, good intentions and appropriate attention then follows this up with the necessary change of attitude and action.

The numerous levels of light and knowledge contained in the Qur'an are a powerful force for human growth and evolvement. Therefore, it is essential for spiritual progress to reflect, ponder upon and remember the Qur'an. Serious intention, repentance and renewal of one's commitment help to retain key aspects and receive effective guidance.

It is recommended to recite the Qur'an with a good voice and according to the original Arabic pronunciations and linguistic rules. When heard in this manner and followed by understanding, reflection and contemplation of the Qur'an's inner meanings, one is exposed to the heavenly lights that are the cause of all that is on earth.

A clear mind and humble heart are necessary for God's words to be effective. Reverence, respect and love of the Qur'an create the necessary conditions for the purification, energising and illumination of the trusting heart. In the presence of the Lord of the universe, all matters of doubt or human insecurities will vanish.

## 1.7 Other Prophetic Messages

From the time of the Prophet Noah and the great flood, there have been numerous prophets and messengers sent to different peoples and cultures, expressing the same truth about human life on earth and the hereafter.

The Qur'an mentions a number of messengers who were known in the Middle East and describes five in particular who had had a big impact upon their cultures: Noah, Abraham, Jesus, Moses and Muhammad. The Qur'an, however, mentions that no people or nations were left without a messenger from amongst themselves to teach and guide them towards salvation.

Many prophets pronounced laws, scriptures and books. The Qur'an makes special mention of David, Enoch, Moses and Jesus. The mischief of priests and some followers of prophets are also mentioned as a warning to future generations. Religions in history have been plagued by deviance caused by selective readings from the scriptures and pronouncements made out of context.

The one sacred Source of all revelations gives all the prophets and messengers equal status as far as the essence of their message is concerned. There are, however, natural historical differences due to the place and culture of people, their state of evolvement and maturity.

All prophets announced the good news of Allah's mercy and governance over all of life, warned against mischief or lack of submission to God's will, and advocated living with modesty, compassion, generosity and justice to the rest of creation. They also reminded humanity from different angles and perspectives of their ultimate accountability and resurrection after death.

## 1.8 Necessity of Faith

Faith and trust in the all-merciful God are required for proper understanding and absorption of the message of Qur'anic revelation. This Book of Treasures will only impact upon those whose hearts are ready to be illumined. The light of the Qur'an is barred from the sceptics and those in denial of the One God.

Many of the Qur'anic messages and revelations have several levels of meanings and depths. Most Arabic speaking people can understand the basic linguistic meaning, while a deeper understanding can touch seekers of truth – and a yet deeper impact awaits those who are absorbed in a life of religious observation and conduct. With a purified, believing heart, the listener can resonate with the insights and wisdom of the revelations.

Adam, in the Qur'an and the Bible, is allegorically described as a heavenly creation higher than the angels. But it was only when he was equipped with the essential spiritual knowledge, was he able to ascend back to paradise. The ropes of this ascent are made from Divine attributes and qualities such as mercy, knowledge, majesty, sanctity and power. Numerous desirable qualities overflow from the sacred essence of God that believers can see to some extent in creation.

Only the purified heart can be guided by faith towards higher levels of spiritual awareness and sensitivity until a level of certainty is reached that brings about God consciousness at all times.

Whoever believes in Allah's purpose and will and acts for the good of mankind and the rest of creation will progress along the spiritual path. Faith and Islam means leaving behind old ways, habits and even home and family. The struggle towards improving one's inner state as well as outer conditions continues throughout one's life. Trust in Allah and living the Qur'an and prophetic teachings without any doubt brings many rewards in one's outer state, as well as an illumined and guided heart.

## 1.9 The Real and Other Realities

Absolute Truth or Reality are Divine attributes and are names of Allah. However, Absolute Truth and Reality manifest in myriad ways and to different extents in creation and human experience. God is the only Truth and Reality and every other entity is a minor reflection of this absolute state.

Allah knows the seen and unseen. Whatever is in the heavens and on earth is sustained and nurtured by Him and eventually returns to him. The revelation of this knowledge comes through a human being — the Prophet — who had the special capacity to connect with the highest and subtlest realms beyond earthly limitations. The Qur'an was revealed by Truth and as the Real.

During our lives, we experience special insights and states of higher consciousness that can be seen as aspects of the hereafter; we may also suffer setbacks and afflictions, comparable to small hells, or enjoy periods of wellbeing and joy, like samples of paradise. Although these states or experiences may be present at all times, we only feel and experience these openings on special occasions. It is like a flash of insight or a special energy that comes upon us.

Divine Reality is the source of whatever seems real in the transient universe. Without veils, God's light is too immense to be recognised at all. Our earthly life shields us from this absolute, awesome splendour.

Life on earth is like a space between what is absolutely perfect and eternally good and that which is hazy and confused. We love that which is boundless and Real, and we can access it through higher consciousness. The more we meditate and reflect upon the essence of earthly realities and truth, the more we are ready for greater exposure to the Real — and absolute Essence. We perfect our worship by remembering the True origin of everything.

## 1.10 Submission to Truth

All of life's experiences are transitory and illusory; therefore, as human beings, we constantly endeavour to find a reliable reference point that may give us stability and lead to contentment and bliss.

The lower self, or ego, is ever restless and has to be occupied. For the ego or self to exist, it must attach itself to an activity or purpose. Eventually it becomes like a thirsty person lost in the desert, chasing mirages. Exhaustion and confusion may lead the lucky wanderer to surrender with good expectation and faith.

Only when we realise our self-delusions and glimpse a spark from the soul, do we begin to reflect deeply upon the nature of the higher self and submit to its truth. The faithful seeker will come to know that the entire purpose of knowledge is awareness of the ever-presence of Allah — the knower of all, who alone is worthy of worship and adoration. Avoiding falsehood and submission to truth brings about transformation and increases access to higher consciousness and inner guidance.

Guided by the illumined heart, the seeker will recognise the lower self and ego as covers for the higher self and soul. Divine guidance can only be accessed via the heart and the soul. God has placed His spirit within us — our soul — and all else are natural temporal veils of Reality and Truth.

God consciousness implies that a person acts justly and appropriately in every aspect of life. We can get closer to the truth by referring all intentions and actions, as much as we can, to the highest level of consciousness. Ultimately, total trust and submission will deliver us from worldly reliance and afflictions. What is with God is eternal; everything else is transitory and false.

## 1.11 Natural Illusions

God's light manifests itself through veils and shadows. The human soul has emerged from the Real, and therefore human beings seek constant reality at all times whilst experiencing a whole range of what is false or true. Illusions conceal the Real and are therefore necessary conditions for existence and creation in the universe. Earthly life itself is a vast number of interlinked causalities that are all short-lived, and therefore elusive. Only God's original light is permanent.

Whatever is on earth or in the heavens will perish. Only the everlasting Perfection of the One shall remain. We all yearn for that absolute Oneness and seek via numerous avenues: knowledge, full awareness, perfect hearing, sight, everlastingness and other attributes. These can be referred to as the face of God, for they link us to the Divine Essence.

In the plant kingdom, the essence of a tree is passed on through the kernel within the seed. The truth of that species carries on through the kernel whilst the cover of the seed was a necessary protection and condition for the survival and integrity of the kernel. The human ego or lower self is such a cover: it veils the soul within the heart. With spiritual growth and evolvement, this false personal identity or ego will vanish naturally and the lower self will submit to the higher. This is the ultimate resting place or state for the ego to be at. This surrender heralds spiritual success.

Human experiences in this life are like moving waves, which widen as they recede from their initial point of occurrence. Each impulse leads to new waves and relates to them. God promises this continuous displacement and movement from the lower to the higher, where whatever is considered to be lost will be replaced by something better For the faithful and diligent seeker of Truth, the ultimate goal is the perfect and sacred face of God, shining above all.

## 1.12 Ever-Present Perfection

Human beings are driven towards improving their physical, material and mental states. While the soul is ever-perfect, the self is driven towards durable perfections at all levels of life's experiences.

Adam was in a perfect state in boundless paradise — and eternally so. However, having only ever known perfection, he did not realise how unique or special the state of grace he was in. It took *shaytanic* distraction and his descent to earth, along with the conflict and challenges of complementary opposites, for him to wilfully ascend back to bliss.

God is eternally perfect and has created in the most perfect fashion. Conscious creation, therefore, is intrinsically driven towards realising perfection at all times and under all circumstances. Human beings have evolved through the stage of seeking survival and earthly maturity and growth. Once they fulfil that, they strive to ascertain life's true meaning and purpose. The only way to arrive there is to acknowledge the ever-presence of the Life-giver, and experience perfection beyond personal evaluations, expectations and judgment. This implies seeing perfection in every moment, irrespective of our relationship with it. Allah is ever-perfect and so is all that emanates from Him.

The believer trusts in the Divine presence and governance at all times, therefore through transformation by worship and God consciousness, one can see the ever-present perfection, irrespective of the event. This is also how the wise and insightful see grace and order, irrespective of what appears as good or bad. The awakened believer confesses by mind and heart that there is no truth except the one and only Truth, the ever-lasting perfection of His Presence — The True Lord of all.

## 1.13 The Qur'an Reveals Itself

The sincere, humble-hearted seeker will understand and assimilate the messages of the Qur'an in small increments that complement each other. At one level, there is much reason, logic and earthly wisdom that needs to be absorbed and mastered. Then there are levels that relate to personal experiences and others to do with group behaviour and social life. Issues pertaining to relationships and leadership also impinge upon quality of life, and affect everyone within a community. There is always a strong thread of reason and wisdom that connects all issues that relate to quality of life on earth, human justice and responsibility.

All earthly events and experiences are relative and changeable. What is good for a healthy person may worsen the illness of a sick person. The state of one's body, mind and heart are different when one is fleeing from fire than when one is about to fall asleep.

Much of the teachings of the Qur'an are similarly contextual and require proper interpretation and relevant application. It is in these domains that the full meaning of the message and its relevance to a particular situation can become clearer by referring to a similar point mentioned elsewhere in the Qur'an. Some verses are clear and precise, whereas others can be fully understood only by reference to other verses that may define the appropriate context. In one instance, for example, the ego or lower self is referred to as something that can never be pure. Another verse, however, encourages the purification of the lower self — by submitting it to the higher.

Through patience, faith and intelligent application, the Qur'an will make perfect sense at all times except when one is looking for fault and confusion.

## Chapter 2

## God's Light

Introduction
2.1  The Supreme Light
2.2  The Incomparable One
2.3  Pervading Essence
2.4  God's Names and Signposts
2.5  Earth's Nursery
2.6  God's Commands
2.7  God's Prohibitions
2.8  Mercy and Forgiveness
2.9  Levels of Awareness
2.10  Remembrance of God
2.11  Trust in God
2.12  Fear and Love of God
2.13  Unity of Actions and Attributes
2.14  The Essential Reference
2.15  Friends of God

# 2

# God's Light

**Introduction**

Allah is the true Reality that enables all created entities to appear for a while as real and independent entities. Allah is beyond what our mind or senses can even begin to describe, define or perceive. Nothing can be associated with Him or is like Him. We can only reflect upon Allah's great qualities and His Attributes, which we aspire to attain as part of our evolvement in consciousness or spirituality.

Allah is the ultimate Divine name expressing Absolute Essence from which all higher Attributes and names emanate. The word Allah covers whatever is known and unknown in the universe. Thus, Lordship, Mercy, Beauty and all perfections are overflows from the Divine Grace and sacred essence of Allah, who remains independent of all qualities or disruptions.

Divine names mentioned in the Qur'an include the 99 Attributes below. Much of the depth of the meanings is lost in translation.

*Al Rabb* – The Lord. *Al Rahman* – The All-Merciful. *Al-Rahim* – The All-Compassionate. *Al-Malik* – The King. *Al-Quddus* – The Most Pure. *Al Salaam* – The Bestower of Peace. *Al-Mu'min* – The Trustworthy. *Al-Muhaymin* – The Protector. *Al-Aziz* – The Mighty. *Al-Jabbar* – The Compeller. *Al-Mutakabbir* – The Supreme Great. *Al-Khaliq* – The Creator. *Al-Bari'* – The Maker. *Al Musawwir* – The Fashioner. *Al-Ghaffar* – The Coverer of all Faults. *Al-Qahhar* – The Subduer. *Al-Wahhab* – The Bestower. *Al-*

*Razzaq* – The Provider. *Al-Fattah* – The Opener. *Al-Alim* – The All-Knowing. *Al-Qabid* – The Restrictor. *Al-Basit* – The Expander. *Al-Khafid* – The One Who Lowers. *Al-Rafi'* – The Exalter. *Al-Mu'izz* – The Honourer. *Al-Mudhill* – The Abaser. *Al-Sami'* – The All-Hearing. *Al-Basir* – The All-Seeing. *Al-Hakam* – The Judge. *Al-'Adl* – The Just. *Al-Latif* – The Subtle. *Al-Khabir* – The All-Cognisant. *Al-Halim* – The Clement. *Al-Adhim* – The Magnificent. *Al-Ghafir* – The All-Forgiving. *Al-Shakur* – The Grateful. *Al-Ali* – The Most High. *Al-Kabir* – The Most Great. *Al Hafidh* – The Preserver. *Al-Muqit* – The Sustainer. *Al-Hasib* – The One Who Satisfies Needs. *Al-Jalil* – The Majestic. *Al-Karim* – The Most Generous. *Al-Raqib* – The All-Vigilant. *Al-Mujib* – The Responder. *Al-Wasi* – The All-Encompassing. *Al-Hakim* – The Most Wise. *Al-Wadud* – The All-Loving. *Al-Majid* – The Most Splendid. *Al-Ba'ith* – The Resurrector. *Al-Shahid* – The Witnessor. *Al-Haqq* – The Absolute Truth. *Al-Wakil* – The Guardian Trustee. *Al-Qawi* – The Most Strong. *Al-Matin* – The Firm. *Al-Wali* – The Patron. *Al-Hamid* – The Praiseworthy. *Al-Muhsi* – The Appraiser. *Al-Mubdi* – The Originator. *Al-Mu'id* – The Returner. *Al-Muhyi* – The Life Giver. *Al Mumit* – The Death Giver. *Al Hayy* – The Ever-Living. *Al-Qayyum* – The All-Sustaining. *Al-Wajid* – The Manifestor. *Al-Ahad* – The Absolute One. *Al-Samad* – The Self-Sufficient. *Al-Qadir* – The Most Able. *Al-Muqtadir* – The All-Powerful. *Al-Muqaddim* – The Expediter. *Al-Mu'akhir* – The Postponer. *Al-Awwal* – The First. *Al-Akhir* – The Last. *Al-Dhahir* – The Manifest. *Al-Batin* – The Concealed. *Al-Barr* – The Benefactor. *Al-Tawwab* – The Most Accepting of Repentance. *Al-Muntaqim* – The Avenger. *Al-Afu* – The Pardoner. *Al-Ra'uf* – The Most Affectionate. *Malik al-Mulk* – The Master of the Kingdom. *Dhul-Jalali wa al-Ikram* – The Master of Majesty and Nobility. *Al-Wali* – The Patron. *Al-Muta'ali* – The Most Exalted. *Al-Muqsit* – The All-Equitable. *Al-Jami* – The Gatherer. *Al-Ghani* – The Rich Beyond Need. *Al-Mughni* – The Enricher. *Al-Mani* – The Preventer. *Al-Darr* – The Bestower of Affliction. *Al-Nafi* – The

Beneficial. *Al-Nur* – The Light. *Al-Hadi* – The Guide. *Al-Badi* – The Originator. *Al-Baqi* – The Everlasting. *Al-Warith* – The Inheritor. *Al-Rashid* – The Most Discerning. *Al-Sabur* – The Patient. *Al-Wahid* – The One.

Allah's will, designs and decrees govern whatever is seen and unseen in the universe. Creation always appears in pairs and as complementary opposites. Every entity in existence is balanced and rooted in its apparent opposite – every 'bad' is connected to a 'good'. His decrees do not change, but individual and societal destinies change according to the paths followed. Human beings desire ease, harmony and contentment, which are the qualities within the soul; with true submission to Allah, all of these attributes can be realised.

Allah is the essence and source of all that exists. Human beings are guided to truth and light according to the extent of their individual readiness and ability to be transformed. The path of enlightenment begins with the intellectual search for the relationship between cause and effect, actions and events and their meanings, and ultimate purpose. The Real One Source behind all actions and attributes, both seen and unseen, will be realised only by transcending all dualities and causalities. To see the One essence at the root of every situation implies seeing total perfection in the moment. This happens when all 'otherness' fades away under the light of 'Oneness'.

Every human being is driven along the path of unity by the original primal desire for happiness. The Qur'an declares that only by remembrance of Allah does the heart become content and thus truly happy. Our real or perceived worldly needs will eventually drive us towards that direction and goal. For example, our need for health drives us to call upon 'The Healer'. Our need for guidance causes us to evoke 'The Guide'. We are in constant need of calling upon one or more of Allah's names but not always with sufficient faith and focus. The Prophet is the best earthly guide who consistently reflects the Universal Guide. The sincere seeker is constantly focused on a Divine Name or Attribute that is needed to bring about equilibrium and harmony in life. Human life can only reach completeness by appropriate intention, timely action and constant trust in Allah's ever-present grace and mercy.

The enlightened believer aspires to the knowledge and consciousness of Allah's Attributes and light in everything and every situation. We aspire to witness Grace in everything that exists. Therein lies the essence of beauty in creation. In truth, there is only Divine light and the universe is shadows, reflections, and veils of this Truth. From Allah's Light creation emerges — by that Light, creation is sustained to experience life on earth and discover the sacred treasure of the soul within the heart, and unto that Light all shall return.

## 2.1 The Supreme Light

God is the essence and source of the entire cosmos, which is created out of a spectrum of lights and consciousness. These lights overflow through a wide band of streams. As visible light is only a part of the electromagnetic wave, so is human consciousness only a small part of supreme consciousness. The universe contains countless varieties of energy and matter that are permeated by the original light and essence from God. The human soul is like a spark that has overflowed from creation and is lodged within the human heart during its earthly lifetime. God is eternally living and His effulgence brings life to all creatures. We all experience life between brackets of birth and death, yet aspire for longevity, for a prolonged life — the light of lights.

In Truth, there is the Supreme Light: there is only Allah and everything else is dependent upon this Truth. The moon derives its light from the sun, and the sun from intense physical and internal chemical reactions and changes. The Divine light is not subject to any cycles of change or reductions. The Divine presence is ever-perfect throughout the cosmos. God is the only one unique Reality, which is self-sustaining and is not subject to any relative issues that we experience on earth. He is utterly incomparable, eternal and ever-present. It is from the Divine light that space and time have manifested to contain earthly experiences. Human spiritual evolvement implies awareness and consciousness of the ever–present dominance and governance of Allah. Thus, it is natural wisdom to submit, yield and accept this perfect truth.

Supreme consciousness, knowledge and sacred powers accompany Allah's original light. Earthly awareness and sentiency are companions to the light that produces life through heat and the movement of molecules and atoms. Supreme light is the light of lights and light upon light.

## 2.2 The Incomparable One

To Allah belongs whatever is in the heavens and the earth. All of creation is within the confines of space and time and is fashioned according to intricate patterns, then set on a course towards their destiny. Allah is not definable, measurable or tangible, yet His attributes and qualities are most desired by all of creation. He witnesses everything known and unknown. He sees and hears everything. He is the Creator and Sustainer of everything. Thus, our senses are derived from His attributes. He is, above all, within all and after all, and His signs are wherever you turn. We are never able to give Allah His due with regard to the immensity of His Majesty, Beauty, Power or Splendour. He is the one unique, incomparable Reality from which all transient realities derive their characteristics. It is like taking on the colour or hue of the Real — in this case Godliness.

The path to understand the Truth and the Real is through admittance of our personal inadequacy, our reliance on the source of mercy and generosity — Allah. Through love of Allah's attributes and qualities, we begin the process of evolvement in consciousness towards awareness of timelessness in the here and now. Allah is ever-present wherever we are. Thus, when we shift our focus and attention from the tangible and discernible world to the subtle world of essence, we establish the personal bridge between the earth and the heavens. Our consciousness will link what is conditioned with personal awareness of pure consciousness. Practising Muslims punctuate their prayers by declaring "Allah-Akbar" — Allah is greater than any description.

We grow mentally and intellectually by exercising reason and wisdom. With faith and constant religious and spiritual practices, we begin to experience the realms beyond earthly dualities and causalities that lie at the shore of the boundless ocean of incomparability, whilst still perched on the shifting sands of relativities.

## 2.3 Pervading Essence

Allah is the omnipotent and omnipresent. His light is the cause of the entire universe and penetrates everything from outside and inside, from before time and after time.

The Divine presence encompasses what is in heavens and earth, as well as what is within the human heart as a soul. Thus, Allah is with every part of creation at all times. The challenge to human beings in this life is realising that Allah is the Master of the Universe and its sole Lord and owner.

This Divine light is the source of life and consciousness. Every entity that has awareness and sentiency experiences an aspect of life and is energised by different levels of consciousness.

Human beings are gifted with the highest levels of awareness and the widest spectrum of life's experiences from the physical to the most subtle of emotions and moral values that lead to God consciousness and enlightenment.

Through self-knowledge, human beings can transcend the lower self and witness the Divine attributes and lights through the soul. In the light of such awesome beauty and majesty, the believer is humbled to submit to this amazing truth and reality and in so doing, gains access to the original abode of Adam — the state of paradise on earth — within the heart.

Wherever one is, God is there and whenever one reflects, God is the source and cause of that reflection. He is the first before any beginning and the last beyond every end. The mind cannot comprehend the Truth of Divine nature; only through a purified heart does the real unveiling begin.

## 2.4 God's Names and Signposts

We humans bridge two spheres of consciousness or evolvement — survival instinct and self-awareness on the one hand, and higher consciousness and spiritual wisdom on the other.

Life and consciousness emanate from Allah's light which envelops the entire universe. The descent of Adam to earth is accompanied by the gift of knowledge and drives that relate to growth, survival, strength and evolvement. This knowledge and these states relate to Divine attributes or names such as the Ever-Living, the All-Knowing, the All-Powerful, the All-Seeing, the All-Hearing, the All-Sustaining and others.

The names, attributes and Divine qualities are like sacred, golden threads that hold the universe along its destiny from beginning to end. The vegetative world is energised by life and the elements of heat, light, moisture, earth and other basic factors. Touched by the power of life, growth and continuity, it spreads out and multiplies. Animals can read signposts such as power, dominance, control, leadership and protection. Human beings can read and respond to higher Divine attributes like patience, love, honesty and sacrifice. The entire universe responds to different names or attributes in different situations according to each living entity's attainable level of consciousness.

Whenever we supplicate to fulfil different needs, we call upon the Bestower of healing, peace, provisions and contentment at heart. Spiritual evolution takes the faithful seeker to the shore of reliable inner security through God consciousness where all His attributes reside. The faithful seeker experiences life and spiritual growth as a delightful journey signposted by Allah's attributes.

## 2.5  Earth's Nursery

In the allegorical story of Adam, it is the awakening of self awareness and mental inquisitiveness that lie at the root of separation from the original state of unity. This newly-awakened state of personal consciousness and identity includes awareness of the boundaries of space-time. Spiritual evolvement occurs due to this self or personal awareness, seeking out a higher level consciousness, which is its source and origin and is the life-source within the heart.

Inner conflict and the rise of ego are natural forces that drive the self to return to the soul and to sacred Oneness. In paradise, Adam had no notion of duality or change due to space and time. The earthly perch is needed in order to realise that truth is eternal and ever-present, and that duality emanates from unity and is balanced by it. Similarly, good health is balanced by illness and so is friendship and enmity. The realisation of Divine presence comes after many dark nights of confusion and cries for help and salvation.

With maturity and wisdom, our appreciation of and desire to embody higher virtues increases and we become more patient, compassionate and wholesome at heart. Driven by the awareness of the earthly limitations of space-time, we aspire to the vistas of boundless horizons of eternal goodness and delights. In spite of the limitations and constrictions of our earthly life, we catch glimpses of our heavenly essence. We count months and years but the Qur'an reminds us that beyond the earthly cocoon, one day is the equivalent to a thousand years on our calendar.

We may think that we have plenty of time and opportunity in the future but God's judgment is instantaneous and its effect upon us is immediate. The faithful seeker is aware of every instant, thus takes responsibility and yields in the most perfect manner to every situation with appropriate reflection, action and God consciousness. We progress as we attempt to go beyond earthly limitations and towards the higher horizons that lie beyond the boundaries of mental limitations as held by the notion of space and time.

## 2.6 God's Commands

While human beings are driven by their desires and needs, there are those exceptional people whose surrender and faith has shown them that Allah's beauty and generosity extends even before asking. These enlightened people have exercised patience and acted selflessly, righteously and according to Truth. It is incumbent upon us to seek a path that increases our self-awareness and responsibility and helps us to reach to higher consciousness. Past mistakes and regrets make believers more aware and alert to the tricks of the lower self, increases their trust in God and their concern and help for others who are in need.

With wisdom, we realise that our own quality of life and wholesomeness improves when we serve others with kindness, generosity and compassion. Spiritually evolved people are able to access the light within their purified hearts and take good actions, with the best of intentions. Mistakes occur due to distraction of the lower self, whilst virtues emanate from the soul.

It is our duty as human beings to be healthy in body, mind and heart and to maintain equilibrium and balance in every situation. The ultimate Divine command is to be a worthy steward on earth, to avoid all evil thoughts or deeds and to act for the good of all, with constant reference to Allah's generosity, forgiveness and infinite mercy. Remembrance of death and the uncertainties and trials of the hereafter is a most effective remedy for waywardness and regrettable distractions.

God commands us to embrace all the desirable qualities that we know are worthy of a good, believing human being, such as kindness, generosity, compassion, patience and steadfastness. People of faith follow the prescriptions of the Qur'an with courage and honesty, and under all circumstances. It is their duty to live according to the religion of Islam and endeavour to rise to the highest possible levels regarding the knowledge of God's ways and will. God consciousness is the constant touchstone and reference to Light.

## 2.7 God's Prohibitions

Given the capacity to reason and to act appropriately, it is ultimate folly to drift along in life with no clear purpose or desirable destiny. Human suffering is caused mainly by the perpetual, illusory distractions of the lower self and its egotistical fantasies. The un-groomed self loves power and dominance and will always mislead us with the vices of its restless nature.

All acts of injustice, self-conceit, arrogance and other regrettable selfish behaviour will only feed the ego and distance us from the inner soul and source of life — Allah's light. The ultimate virtue arises when the lower self becomes transparent and ready to surrender to its soul.

Individually and collectively, we need to refrain from corruption, wasteful behaviour and any intention or action that hardens the heart and makes us forget the transience of life on earth. The self needs to be restrained and groomed with cautious awareness of every intention and action.

It is important to remember that God knows and is aware of whatever we think or do. The worst disease that can afflict us is the sick heart that veils the soul's light, prevents it from reaching the mind, blocking out proper reflection and awareness of self-accountability.

Creation was brought about for the purpose of knowing Allah

and to live fully within God consciousness. Every human mistake can be overcome and forgiven, except lack of belief in or knowledge of the all-encompassing, universal Lord and Master — Allah, the supreme and unique God. The ultimate sin is to forget the sacred light of Oneness that holds the universe and enables us to experience life.

## 2.8 Mercy and Forgiveness

Allah is ever-generous, forgiving and merciful. He does not punish anyone for their misdeeds. We do, however, feel the backlash of our own wrong actions. Through religious discipline and practice, we begin to see and experience the mystery of the Divine presence and its power. This sacred presence is always perfect and can be accessed through trust and higher consciousness of the soul.

In our human limitations and inadequacy, we desire reassurance, forgiveness and loving care — glorious qualities that God radiates. He created out of love, in order to be known and adored through proper worship. Indeed, the human story is that of evolvement along the path of being absorbed in the Divine light of transcendence. By expecting the best from Allah, we shall experience perfection on earth.

As human beings, we are bracketed between the lower self and the sacred soul. Through faith, prayers and will, we can experience God's mercy, love, appropriate guidance and wholesome outcome. We all make mistakes in our lives that we regret, and only through Allah's generosity and forgiveness, we are not immediately held accountable. It is as though God postpones admonishment of our wrong actions so that we may still correct our ways before it is too late.

By being compassionate, forgiving, kind and generous to the rest of creation, we open our hearts to the Divine beams of mercy and infinite generosity. To bring about goodness and happiness, we need to act with good intentions and generosity; to bring about light; we need to turn away from all shadows and darkness. Allah's light encompasses all shadows and colours, known and unknown. Our level of intention and attention will be reflected back to us as our inner state.

## 2.9 Levels of Awareness

Absolute or sacred light is non-discernible and is beyond the space-time limitation. Pure consciousness accompanies pure light. The vast spectrum of consciousness emanates from pure consciousness and is experienced at different levels and degrees similar to how we experience light and colour.

Human consciousness is discerned through two main levels or spheres of awareness. There is the personal, local or conditioned consciousness and the boundless, pure consciousness that enables us to go beyond the limitations of local awareness.

The fall (or the expulsion) of Adam from paradise and the knowledge that he was given of the great attributes and qualities that the soul has and knows are the propelling forces for all human beings to seek the perfect state at all times and in every situation. The ultimate treasure, gift or 'loaned trust' implies pure consciousness that is boundless and eternal, as the human soul.

Humanity shares local or personal awareness that produces empathy, sympathy and many other helpful emotions and feelings. It is awareness of awareness that distinguishes human beings from other humanoids and it is probably a function of the frontal lobe, which may be the physiological sign of the rise of Adam (or his descent from paradise).

Human beings are driven to higher consciousness by prayer, meditation and a host of creative pursuits such as arts, music and other transcendental activities, reflecting our yearning to return to a blissful state of contented happiness: paradise. It is ultimately supreme consciousness that we all desire.

## 2.10 Remembrance of God

God is the light and source, or essence, of everything known and unknown. It is due to that Light and Pure Consciousness that light and consciousness permeate existence. The human soul has imbibed this primal state of pure "beingness", as well as "somethingness", or self. Thus, the individual self evolves toward the realisation of its essence or soul both through mind and meditation as well as spiritually through the purified heart.

The soul energises the baby to grow according to its intrinsic genetic programme. The earthly evolution of life from a single cell onward over a period of millions of years is echoed in all living creatures. The mind began to develop and grow, linking the physiological, biological side with the subtler essence referred to as consciousness or life force. Personal experiences and memories grow and develop, producing changes in personality and identity, all of which is dependent upon the soul. Forgetfulness is perhaps as healthy as remembrance of events, yet the drive toward pre-consciousness or remembrance of what was there before memory, space and time is relentless. We strive to remember Allah's original light. We will not be secure until we realise that Allah is the source or essence of all life.

God consciousness is a quality of the soul, but the self has to realise that worldly limitations can only be transcended by the heart via a pathway that is different to that of worldly pursuits and endeavours. God knows Himself and is always in complete remembrance of Himself. We can access that zone through transcendence of limitations, by invocation of higher consciousness. Ultimately, it is by God's mercy and grace alone that we experience the original state of blissful awareness of the Perfect Paradise where Adam was created in the first place.

## 2.11 Trust in God

It is part of our human nature to exercise reason and logic, to learn the patterns of causalities and to try to understand how objects connect with each other and relate to energy and other forces. We are inquisitive about the outer universe; we seek the unknown and are very concerned about death and what follows it. We often discuss the nature of God and ways to understand Him better, but while we know that the universe is energised by the unifying power of God, we often feel lonely, restless and uncertain. We need living faith.

Often, in the beginning, our trust in God can be superstitious and while this may be of some help initially, it is only a starting point to spiritual insights and openings of certainty and enlightened trust for the serious seeker. Hope and good expectations of God's generosity will undoubtedly bring about desirable outcomes. Through living faith, we are guided towards unquestionable belief in God's perfect mercy and receive appropriate direction.

The lower self always asserts itself and presumes independence and freedom from its soul within the heart. The reflective seeker uses rationality and intellect up to the point of insights and spiritual lights. Our limited human consciousness must take us through all discernable patterns until it reaches the point of higher consciousness. We start by trusting reason and mind but need to reach the zone of heart and soul to establish real trust.

Although trust and faith in God can begin blindly, its end may be fully illumined and based on personal experience and certainty. An honest connection between reason and insights are necessary for trust to become the rudder that drives us along our life's journey along visible earthly paths, as well as unseen regions towards our destiny.

## 2.12 Fear and Love of God

The soul is bounded by love, trust and total submission to God. Human life and consciousness, however, is subject to the natural laws of duality. We therefore experience both fear (pain) and love (joy), relating to the repulsion and attraction, which are the driving forces for growth in consciousness. Fear of pain and loss of what is desirable is always accompanied by love of attaining what is desirable. Fear also relates to self-concern, self-image and all other egotistic tendencies, whereas love brings about freedom from the lower self and lightness of heart. We dislike fear and we, therefore, tend to avoid it. We prefer love and we are driven toward it. They are the key complementary opposites that include life and death; good and bad.

Fear causes constriction, whereas love relates to freedom and expansion. Fear is a necessary condition for basic survival while love is essential for growth and evolvement. They balance each other to achieve a wholesome drive in life. Divine love, however, covers all earthly loves and fears.

There are several levels or degrees of fear and love. The first level is to do with the rise of the lower self. The highest is to do with God. We fear missing His presence, or eternal light, and love attaining unity with our soul — His light within the heart.

Allah loves all of His creation and it is up to us to learn how to love Him and bring about the transformation that will alter our mental attitudes so that we can clearly feel the results in our lives. In order to realise God's unconditional love, the love of the soul, we have to develop the necessary discipline, to trust in Allah's mercy and constancy, to do good deeds, to be accountable, reflective and adhere strictly to moral values and virtues.

## 2.13 Unity of Actions and Attributes

We try to create situations that bring about relief, ease and comfort with our physical actions. No action is possible without applying an appropriate form or force of energy. As the source of all energies is the same, then all actions emanate from One Source and, as such, are unified at inception. We have the illusion, however, that we act independently from the universal Source from which all energies are drawn, but in reality, all actions are unified in essence.

All desirable attributes emanate from Allah and are imprinted upon the soul. Life, power, wealth, knowledge, strength, excellence and many other qualities are like beams of light whose origin is Allah's light. Thus all great attributes are united in essence — One Essence.

God's attributes appear to be different from each other as they signify different aspects of experience, but following them to their root, we reach the one original, sacred Source. The all-knower is also the all-powerful and the Lord of all. These attributes and our need to realise or experience them is like the sacred net that captures creation.

Unity at essence envelops all other levels of connections relating to attributes or actions. What appears to be diverse and different is held together, in essence, by the sacred, unifying field of the Lord of creation. This is the reason for the declaration that there is no God except The God and everything emanates from and is held by the same Reality and Truth.

Life's purpose is fulfilled when we look for the threads or connections that emanate from the Divine essence and return to it to complete the loop of descent and ascent from the garden of perfect unity.

## 2.14 The Essential Reference

Our search for Truth and the Real is a deeply rooted quest for something that is secure, constant and everlasting. The human soul is constant and is in residence for a while within the heart. This sacred soul is the ever-present personal reference in all situations for guidance and steadiness along our journey.

Created in God's image, the human soul or spirit represents the One and the Real. It knows all the Divine qualities and transmits these towards the body and mind as clearly as the extent of purity of the heart allows. Through wisdom and spiritual training, one learns that to benefit from these virtues, the ego has to submit to the soul and enjoy all the positive delights of faith and spiritual progress.

All of our experiences have a transient reality that leave a trace in our memory for a while. The human mind is designed to facilitate worldly functions and to enable a connection between body and soul. Residing in the heart, the soul is like a personal God and connects with the physical and material realms through the mind, the senses and the complex nervous system. Through the mind and the senses, we experience countless situations with various qualities and quantities.

To experience the Real and ever-constant, we need to transcend all the shifting shadows and mirages of transient realities. All outer experiences are veils emerging and receding back to the Real. There is none other than the Real — Allah — and the purpose of life is to realise this sacred truth and thereby be liberated from all falsehoods and illusions.

## 2.15 Friends of God

With maturity and spiritual evolvement, the human being will begin to realise the falsehood of all earthly experiences and the idea of separate and independent personal identity.

The illusion of space and time, and the experience of separation of existence and its distance from the Divine essence enables the ego and mind to grow until such time that faith and spiritual progress enables one to resonate with the unifying light of God. When the lower self has totally surrendered to the soul, which is a reflector of the Divine soul — Allah — then pure love, inner security and passionate absorption in the One Essence prevails.

Human drives are largely based upon fear for what we hold dear but may be lost, and desires or needs that have to be fulfilled. These fears and desires are created in the lower levels of consciousness and are the main obstacle to spiritual evolvement.

Sorrow, sadness and depression are emotions that relate to the ego or the lower self. By using reason and intellect, even the most undesirable situation can be explained and understood as a natural though unfortunate event. Awakened beings have the least fears or sorrows; they see events for what they are, without it affecting their hearts.

Friendship of God begins with the desire for attributes carried by the soul. As the faithful seeker of truth begins to lose the egotistic identity, the realisation of the presence of Divine Reality increases that friendship and love to the point where there will be hardly any grief or worldly concerns. Piety, supplication, remembrance of Allah and all other acts of righteousness and virtues will ultimately lead to total absorption, in perfect contentment, with the glorious Beloved.

# Chapter 3

## Creation

Introduction
3.1  Emergence of the Universe
3.2  God's Universe
3.3  God's Will and Purpose
3.4  This and Other Realms
3.5  Naturally in Transition
3.6  Substances and Energy
3.7  Dualities and Other Reflections
3.8  Angels, *Jinn* (invisible beings) and Demons
3.9  Human Evolution
3.10  Individuals and Groups
3.11  In a Direction
3.12  Capacity and Readiness
3.13  Orbits and Cycles Within a Whole

# 3

# Creation

**Introduction**

The beginning of creation is a mystery often described as a sacred command: to be. From utter unity and nothingness, an explosive cosmic expansion and diversity came about. Countless stars and galaxies vibrate, circulate and orbit in an extraordinary dynamic and interactive way, and a similar invisible world exists within the atoms. Early on in creation splitting and dispersion was the dominant force in bringing about our known universe and others unknown to us. The Qur'an describes the end of time and the collapse of the universe back to its original nothingness. The solid mountains return to dust and all of creation back to the mysterious unity of Essence, or Absolute Oneness.

Allah is the Master and Lord of all the worlds and all that is known or unknown in the heavens and earth. He is the Great, the Mighty, the Merciful, and the Creator of the heavens and earth and all that is between them. All entities of this world and the hereafter, good and evil, the fire and the garden, angels, prophets and messengers emanate from Him. Everything overflows from Him, is sustained by Him and in the end returns to Him. Yet God Himself remains unaffected and is beyond descriptions and perceived perfections. Allah is the absolute Truth and is not comparable to anything, whereas all human comprehension is relative and changeable.

All creation exists in pairs and opposites. All human experiences reflect this reality. With birth comes death, light shows darkness, good is connected to bad, heaven to earth, knowledge to ignorance and health to illness. Human beings need to discover the ways of nature in order to work alongside its patterns so that harmony may be achieved and maintained. The Qur'an describes Allah's creational designs and intentions so that we may submit to His blueprint and follow His programme. To reflect upon nature, its understandable as well as its unusual ways, is essential for human survival and spiritual evolvement.

The physical world is only a small portion of total creation – it's like the tip of an iceberg. The unseen is far greater than that which appears solid and physical. The Qur'an describes the seven layers of heavens and earth, angelic powers, the *Jinn* (spirits) and other energies, as well as the disruptive satanic forces. It emphasises the immensity of the unseen compared to that which we discern through our senses and minds.

Our world is primarily experienced and understood through causal dynamics and rational analysis. One action leads to another and may correlate with other events. Human endeavour is motivated by the desire for happiness, which implies desirelessness, contentment and peace. The ultimate human achievement is to have a pure heart with living faith, unconditional passionate love for Allah. Education and knowledge are essential and helpful for one to surrender to His ever-flowing mercy and perfections.

The physical and material world – as well as the world of actions and causality – is all held together by His unity, which can be perceived by deep reflection, meditation and witnessing what is the essence of all. All discernible realms follow patterns and laws that relate to the dominion of Divine qualities and attributes that operate as subtle unifying beams and threads of energy within creation. The universe is like a womb whose fabric is space-time and is supported by the invisible threads of Oneness.

Divine unity in essence is the most subtle and mysterious of truths. All of Allah's creation is dependent on His light or Essence and is sustained by it and to it, all returns. The whole of creation simply emits signs and signals that point to the One Creator.

## 3.1 Emergence of the Universe

From the state of the absolute and non-discernable unity, almost countless, diverse entities began to emerge. From the unseen invisible God, multitudes of universes and creations began to appear according to special cycles and patterns.

On earth, life began to evolve and multiply from the humble start of semi-permeable cells. The Adamic emergence is the culmination of creation's evolution — a new level of consciousness that supersedes all of creation.

That original unified state began to disperse as countless interlinked celestial entities and creatures, as well as terrestrial bodies composed of matter and energy. From the invisible and non-discernable original essence a wide range of possibly different entities emerged, all to be contained within the womb of time and space. Thus, any living entity in creation can be referred to with regards to a position within time and space and its particular lifespan.

The explosive emergence of the universe and celestial materials remains a great mystery. Our minds cannot imagine how everything emerged from nothingness. The entire universe is floating within multitudes of orbits and spheres, energised and led by the original essence to follow certain patterns and directions.

The original, intangible unity gave way to infinite varieties of discernable entities with boundaries and limitations. The original Divine light remains exactly as it was before creation — ever-perfect and unaffected by whatever occurs in the cosmos. All seen and unseen forces in creation remain within a prescribed direction and limitations on a journey back to the origin.

## 3.2 God's Universe

Within the universe, we can easily discern different levels of creation and we often classify different entities as earthly material or basic living cells, plants, insects, animals and humans. Anything that is sentient is generally considered as a living entity but we tend to have more connections with creations that demonstrate consciousness. It is only human beings and, to a lesser extent some apes, that show some degree of self-awareness and wider consciousness. God's universe spans extreme ends of speed, heat, calmness, explosiveness and all that can be imagined by us humans.

The evolutionary direction of awareness and consciousness seems to be toward the discovery of the origin of life and the way it operates. Human beings are especially driven to discover the will of the Creator and Master of the Universe. This knowledge was revealed to prophets, who presented religions as maps and codes of conduct for a safe journey to the next life, which is the ongoing consciousness of the individual soul after death in this body.

Duality does not only exist in the earthly realm. God has mirrored this world with the hereafter, and thus there are two sets of gardens and hells. What we experience within space-time on earth will be realised fully in the hereafter. In that zone, space and time only faintly resemble their earthly equivalents.

Thousands of years may flicker by instantly and vast spaces may shrink to insignificant distance. God controls numerous kingdoms and diverse domains.

The Qur'an gives us the metaphor that the heavens and earth are in God's palm. Therefore, His power and light permeate the universe where human beings have the potential for higher consciousness, to realise the supreme presence and governance.

## 3.3 God's Will and Purpose

Every entity in creation has limitations within its nature, but aspires to reach its ultimate potential. If every creation follows its natural primal design, it will flow with ease within the boundaries of birth and death in this life. Human beings love ease and comfort — this is the natural state of the soul within the heart and not the restless self.

The egotistic self is a shadow of the soul and is not independent. It is there to complete the illusion of the separation of the self from soul. With maturity and wisdom, man realises that it is this ego-self that veils his true identity — the soul. Thus, the lower self or ego has surpassed its purpose to drive us towards God consciousness through soul awareness.

God's will and purpose in life is engrained within the human soul and is enacted through the dual nature of human consciousness. Biological evolution and the need of love of survival and growth is the foundation upon which spiritual evolution takes place. First, the ego develops, then it has to surrender to the soul. The limited and conditioned consciousness of the lower self is intended to lead to higher consciousness and enlightenment.

The ultimate purpose in this life is to realise the original and ever-present, perfect, sacred light behind and within everything in creation. To see and understand dualities as projected images and shadows upon the screen of Divine unity is the purpose of life. It is rational and intelligent to discern different entities and realities. It is enlightenment to know the ever-present unifying power of Allah within the universe. The mind is designed to see in sets of two and discriminate for practical earthly purposes, namely survival. The heart is where the soul resides. It is the soul that knows the true and Real One. All human hopes, aspirations and desires can only be satisfied by realising God through the light of the soul. God's will is for us to know His presence through all His Beauty, Majesty and Effulgence.

## 3.4 This and Other Realms

Human beings experience several states or realms within our consciousness such as the normal everyday world, dream world, the subconscious and levels of creative and imaginal consciousness.

Basic human consciousness is a stream that emanates from and returns to higher consciousness. The limitation and localisation of personal consciousness leads toward the horizon of greater consciousness. Our life on earth is like a perch from which we strive towards wider vistas. The material side of creation tends to dominate or veil the unseen or intangible realities, although all matter are forms of energy that have been frozen for a while.

The original, absolute One and essence of all creation is the source of all creation and consciousness. The spectrum of light and consciousness are immense in their width and breadth and are the source of all energies, which give rise to matter, anti-matter and all that is seen and unseen within the universe. All human cognisance is as a result of contrasting or matching dualities, which can be specific and easy to define or broad and wide in content. As human beings, we experience different multitudes and levels of consciousness such as that of the wakeful state, sleep, dream or hallucination. In broad terms, there is also the realm of the earthly world and that which comes after the soul departs from its earthly shield of body and mind.

The hereafter is where the worldly forms may appear as faint shadows and their inner quality stands out. On earth, everything is relative and transient but in the hereafter, all of our measures and values become insignificant.

Hence, our world is like a nursery and preparatory ground for what is beyond. For the enlightened beings, the next world is seen as here and now, whereas most people postpone reflection upon Truth and Reality.

## 3.5 Naturally in Transition

The drama of life unfolds in three stages. First is birth; then comes maturity and growth, and the third and most dramatic act is that of death and return to the origin. The middle portion, namely maturity and growth, is what occupies our attention most. This long transition is where we most need guidance and direction so that we reconcile with the destiny that awaits us.

Our daily life is full of challenges and uncertainties as we pursue activities balanced between attractions and repulsions or what is considered good or bad. We love security and seek constant joy whilst we know that no earthly experience is permanent. Everything in this life is naturally changeable and there is nothing absolutely constant.

We know that nature itself is the arena of changes and cycles. No two days are the same and no experience is ever exactly repeatable. Yet, we all seek what is sustainably good. In this hope, people have an advantage over others, especially during difficult times.

Rationally, we understand and accept the transiency of our life on earth. Every goodness is tinted with its opposite. People of faith regard perfect goodness as a Divine quality that is only reflected in the purified heart. The soul within the heart knows Allah's lights and colours and thereby gives the earthly journey stability and direction and reduces outer securities and doubts thereby fade.

The earth is the transit lounge for the children of Adam, whose souls have descended from the heavens and will return back to the original abode after leaving all earthly shadows and veils behind, disentangling the soul from its material position.

## 3.6 Substances and Energy

God's light is the essence and primary cause of the universe and all other forms – energy, matter and consciousness – are derivatives of this light.

The most prevalent and essential entities for life on earth are water, air, wind and fire, which our human senses are geared towards. The hot, the cold, the dry and the wet, as well as all smells, tastes, feelings and other sensations relate to these substances. All animals and creatures adapt to different appropriate relationships with these substances and thus have their lives regulated and adapted accordingly.

Light is accompanied by consciousness, otherwise Light cannot be experienced. Human nature is distinguished by double consciousness: limited and conditioned, and that which is pure and beyond limitations. Our physical structure is based on earthly materials or energy, energised by personal and conditioned consciousness whilst heart and soul connect to the higher consciousness.

We become aware of consciousness itself when it is lost temporarily, as in sleep or fainting. It is like breathing; we realise how dependent we are on air, when we are deprived of it. The fish in the ocean take water for granted and are not even aware of it. We too assume that air will be there every morning when we wake.

Matter is only a form of energy temporarily held in a certain shape, which identifies it for a period of time before it returns back to the energy pool. All of life occurs within fields of interactive cells and substances that are energised by subtler forces. From the perfect unseen, the visible and tangible world gives us countless examples of possible combinations of blueprints. These have all emerged to illustrate the immense possibility that can be derived from the vast boundlessness of the Essence. Allah is beyond measure; substances and energies overflow from His light.

## 3.7 Dualities and Other Reflections

All of creation exists in pairs and all human experiences have two aspects with complementary opposites — like two sides of a coin. There can't be goodness without badness connected to it, or attraction without repulsion. For every sickness, there is a remedy and for every order, there is disorder. Love's dark side is hate, so is hell to paradise and bad to good. Adam had to descend to earth and experience all the opposites to struggle back to the perfection of the timeless harmony of paradise.

There are numerous levels and layers of mirror images of entities, dualities and pluralities. There is a wide range of hardness and softness in the tangible world. The same examples can be seen in all other matters of senses and feelings. Creation appears in pairs and symmetries that show different degrees of opposite qualities as well as complementarities.

The lights emerging from the One essence spread out throughout the universe to reveal countless qualities and multiple shadows, forms and shapes. It is a constant human quest to discover the roots, origin and the relationships between these diversities and dualities. We also look for causalities and correlation in the endeavour of reaching a conclusion that is secure and holds true. In the outer world, there is no permanent stability as everything is naturally subject to change in time and space. What is a poison for a certain condition is a cure in another and what is desirable now can be despised later. The children of Adam have to battle on earth under the shade of the tree of discord and dispersion. Only by transcendence do we start on the desirable journey of ascendance back to the sacred realm of true security.

Most worldly quests are like chasing after a mirage that only appears to be water, but cannot really quench thirst. It disappears to reappear at another time. Those who follow a religious or spiritual map, with demarcated outer boundaries and limitations, and practice constant reflection and self-correction are on the path of transcending the confusions of lower consciousness to the delights of God consciousness and Oneness.

## 3.8 Angels, *Jinn* (invisible beings) and Demons

There are many intangible creations (classically named as *Jinn*, angels or satans) that occasionally connect with us in mysterious ways. These are mostly energy entities that have their patterns of life and boundaries. Human consciousness is potentially able to conceive much of what is on earth and can have some idea about what is beyond. We evolve from discerning mostly the physical sensations to subtler mental, intellectual and spiritual domains.

Angels are described as having different levels of power and complexity and act like special energy packets or forces with clear tasks or objectives. It is mostly archangels that had impacted upon prophets to produce revelations and miraculous deeds. Angels connect with humans at levels beyond the mind and senses — closer to the sixth sense or a hazy dream. They don't have a free will or the higher levels of consciousness that we can access.

Angels interact with more material creation to affect our human quality of life. They follow sets of patterns and pathways of action beyond our mental logic or reason; they solely act out God's Will.

*Jinn* are similar creatures to human beings except that their main substance is fire instead of earth, as is the case of humans. They are unseen and are in locations tucked away from human beings, although their proximity can be felt on special occasions. When they heard the Qur'an, some of them submitted to its truth and others (like humans) rejected it. The social life and hierarchy of *Jinn* is not dissimilar to that of human beings. The Prophet Solomon had power over them, but the conventional wisdom is not to be concerned or involved with these and other 'magical' and unseen creations.

Satan, Iblis, the devil or other demonic entities relate to the dark side of human life and its negative aspects that impede spiritual progress. It was the satanic energy that disturbed Adam's perfect state of bliss in the Garden by mental arousal and inquisitiveness about the tree of eternity or state of eternity.

## 3.9 Human Evolution

The state of Adam in paradise was that of pure beingness and bliss, and the descent to earth symbolises the conscious rise and return (by personal will and the grace of God) back to the state of paradise. The growth and development of mankind on earth is at a physiological level as well as in consciousness. Thus, at the level of biological evolution we are not too dissimilar from other animals.

The behaviour of a human has much in common with that of an ape. It is with the development of the mind, after a few years, that the second level of evolution begins. This is marked with the rise of the intellect and the search of higher meaning in life, self-knowledge and other moral or religious matters. It is here that human beings are radically different from other animals. This double evolution echoes two spheres of consciousness; one is conditioned and local and relates to personal identity and personality, the other relates to higher consciousness or transcendence.

The favoured position of Adam is a metaphor for the evolving homo sapiens' ability to be aware of awareness, self-account-ability and responsibility. It is only human beings who can realise the difference between a personal view and understanding and someone else's values, and the ability to change these views. Human beings have two heritages: one is a physical and material evolution spanning millions of years, the other a spiritual one and is in itself not subject to time and effort.

God's will and power is the constant true light that beckons us all unto it. Soul consciousness and access to its unitive state follows after awareness and control of ego consciousness and its insufficiency — giving rise to reconnection between self and soul. It is the dual evolution that gives the human beings the opening to Oneness.

## 3.10 Individuals and Groups

Most animals live in groups of varying numbers with particular behavioural patterns suitable for that specie. For survival as well as growth and evolvement, this grouping and connectedness is essential. In the case of human beings, the family, peer relationships and other societal groupings are essential for growth in consciousness towards the highest potential. Initially, we have emerged from one family with one natural language but as we spread out on the earth in different regions, climates and environments, our habits, skills and survival needs varied — thereby producing different cultures and languages. Outwardly there appear to be countless differences in shape, size, colour, and behaviour, but once we look to the human inner state, we find that we are all the same in our drive toward wellbeing of body, mind, heart and durable happiness.

Throughout our lifetime, we move from one desire or need to another and thereby pursue actions or projects that give us tangible satisfaction. The believer in God pursues a path that leads to the realisation of the original source of creation, Allah, the One eternal source of life. For the enlightened being, outer differences fade away and otherness disappears when the light of Oneness shines; when the sun of truth is bright, all stars disappear. Therefore, if only one person awakens due to the mirror and light of another, then it is as though all of creation has come to life. Also the unjust killing of another self is like killing all of mankind.

The quality and strength of a group is more than the sum total of its individual member's capacity or power. A wayward and distracted individual may cause damage and loss to one or more persons but a society that is breaking up will bring about major chaos and death to many. An individual who brings about destruction upon oneself is like somebody dying of a heart attack, whereas community mob frenzy may cause explosive destructiveness. There is constant resonance between individuals and their social group.

### 3.11 In a Direction

Every entity on earth pursues a direction and purpose in every moment. As human beings, we can trace the threads of the ultimate purpose — back to original unity. Our outer desires, needs and projects change constantly yet our inner love for ease, comfort and happiness is persistent. All needs or paths ultimately lead to the door of blissfulness and contentment. The seeker of paradise hopes to experience aspects of it on earth to be further encouraged with practice and good expectations of the ultimate paradise.

Every sentient creature on earth moves along a direction that leads to a higher state of consciousness or self-awareness. Although life on earth seems to have evolved in a random fashion, the directionality of desire for the highest possible state of consciousness is clear in evolved animals — especially man.

The soul within the heart draws its power directly from the Omnipresent. For outer direction, we take counsel from others and for the inner we simply need to turn to the heart and the sacred Light therein. All actions have their essence in Allah and so are all desirable attributes — they belong to God and emanate from Him. That original sacred Light is the beacon that everything is directed towards.

Clarity of intention is essential to call upon and resonate with an appropriate attribute. We need to narrow down what we are looking for and enter through that binary gate. It is closed for dead hearts and open for humble and pure hearts. To seek power is different from desiring healing; to seek peace is different from asking for good companionship. These are different threads, but all lead to the same source – that is the ultimate destination of gatheredness and unification. The universe, which is defined within space and time, is speedily returning to the vanishing point of nothingness.

## 3.12 Capacity and Readiness

Differences in our values are both qualitative and quantitative. A small variation in temperature or humidity could be decisive as far as life or death of a fragile mould cell is concerned. Simple entities have considerable restrictions and limitations that give them certain advantages as well as disadvantages. With more developed and evolved creatures, the range of abilities increases until we reach the human being who has the capability of life on earth with all its restrictions and limitations, as well as the constant desire to return to the celestial realm beyond time and space. Adam and his offspring are endowed with minds and organs that enable them to live and function with limited consciousness, whilst carrying a soul that contains pure consciousness and boundless horizons. It is this latter capacity that needs to be reached, otherwise we remain unfulfilled. The capacity for transcendence is there with all human beings but the readiness to experience higher consciousness needs personal determination, will and application of God's commands and prohibitions.

It is natural that during youth most of our activities relate to conditioned consciousness and biological growth. With age and wisdom, the connection between lower and higher consciousness strengthens until that lower consciousness matters least and soul consciousness dominates. Spiritual evolution implies this state.

Perfecting worship begins when the highest attributes of God are seen in day-to-day situations. At this stage, one sees how every creation is exercising its appropriate expression of adoration of God. A fulfilled life is when our capability and capacity are fully utilised and we experience unity in what appears as diverse and different in the outer world. An enlightened being witnesses perfection and Divine grace in all situations.

## 3.13 Orbits and Cycles Within a Whole

Everything in creation has its particular character that gives it its special identity and its outer boundaries, limitations, extent and hierarchy of connections and dependencies. Every atom, molecule, or piece of crystal broadcasts its frequency or variable vibrations at different states. Complex systems emit multitudes of vibrations and oscillating parts and are linked to each other in obvious or subtle ways.

The human body is like a microcosm that mirrors aspects of the entire macrocosm. The millions of tiny living bacteria within the human being defy accurate estimation or comprehension. The human being is like a walking mini cosmos with countless systems and sub-systems responding to subtle means of communications.

The human mind and heart has the capacity to be attuned with numerous levels of consciousness. Special insights or intuition are due to reception of special signals that are not common or usual.

The four seasons on earth and the constant changes in celestial and terrestrial cycles and orbits are manifestations of the countless variations in vibration and subtle interactions, which are often not perceptible by us. This apparent deficiency in us is a natural protection that sets outer boundaries within our human (lower) consciousness.

Everything within the universe fits or acts within its domain as part of the pulsating, living whole. The human soul has the capacity to resonate fully with the Master and Creator of the Cosmos. It is up to individuals to use their reasoning and intellect fully, and then to refer to the highest consciousness, which is the soul within the heart. The human mind and lower self is only alive due to the life that radiates from soul.

# Chapter 4

## Adam and Human Nature

Introduction
4.1  Adam in Paradise
4.2  Descent and Ascent of Adam
4.3  Acting Stewardship
4.4  Human Composition
4.5  Sublime and Ridiculous
4.6  Mind, Body and Soul
4.7  Author of Fate
4.8  Punishment and Reward
4.9  Vices of the Self
4.10  Virtues of the Soul
4.11  The Wholesome Heart
4.12  To Witness and Transcend
4.13  Decree and Destiny
4.14  The Complete Person
4.15  Full Consciousness

# 4

# Adam and Human Nature

**Introduction**

The Qur'an gives us several allegorical descriptions of the story of Adam and his abode in the heavenly paradise. It describes his creation, his relationships to angels, his descent to earth, his purpose in life and it gives a prescription to his offspring for their subsequent return to paradise. The Qur'an describes the early dramatic events of Adam's apparent errors (mostly due to self-consciousness and separation from Oneness) and subsequent knowledge of the Creator through admission of shortcomings and subsequent realisation of the truth of Oneness through Divine attributes, discrimination, reason and insights.

There is one original blueprint of humanity from which all selves have come. The forces of attraction and repulsion drive the human self towards many levels of fulfilment culminating with the recognition of the soul within and thereby prevalence of the Divine light. If we submit and aspire to the higher self and act appropriately, we will awaken to wisdom and knowledge that will lead us to the ultimate goodness. On the other hand, if we fall into the pitfalls of the lower self, then disillusionment, confusion and unhappiness will be the result. Human awareness of the lower tendencies is the driving force towards higher qualities and virtues that are latent within us, at heart. There is a natural drive towards enlightenment that needs to be followed – away from the lower tendencies and egotism.

The number and types of seekers of truth, their religions,

culture, and racial background is beyond count but their desired destination is similar. The determined truthful seekers will transcend the lower self and reach a favourable destiny. The lower self or ego seeks ease, pleasure and power, whereas the soul possesses all these qualities and more. Once a being is illumined with the knowledge of the All-Encompassing God, His unity, His ever-presence and His Perfections, then these lower tendencies will be replaced by illumination, inner light and witnessing. This is the interplay between the lower self and its perfect soul within the heart. This sacred soul carries the imprint of Allah's qualities and names and can be regarded, as God's Presence within the heart.

Human beings seek a destiny of durable contentment, peace and happiness. The path to this end is that of submission (*Islam*) to the innate driving force of faith (*iman*) in God's generosity, mercy and forgiveness. We need to maintain great caution from the dangers of outer distractions (*taqwa*) in order to be attuned to higher consciousness and awareness of Divine presence and dominance. The perfection of this transformation is faultless and leads to the ultimate transaction (*ihsan*) – total awareness of God's presence and guidance to pure consciousness that supersedes but does not obliterate other levels of awareness of experience.

Prophets have taught that he who knows himself knows his Lord. Self-knowledge is, therefore, the foundation of spiritual progress and evolvement. The human soul belongs to the realm of subtle lights and Divine Reality but interacts with physical matter, the mind and the changing body. It is the source of life and consciousness. The Qur'an calls it a Sacred Breath. The human position on earth is the bridge and interspace between this world and the world of the unseen beyond the limitations of space and time. As our essential nature is spiritual light, we yearn constantly for the perfect and boundless realm of absolute goodness and perfection — paradise. We often resent our temporary exile on earth due to the soul's memory of the eternal garden.

In childhood, the main pre-occupation is to nurture the young body and to develop its physiology, mental capacity and senses. However, with maturity and experience, the self looks for additional nourishment and guidance from the intellect and insights from the soul. The wise person moves from total identification with the body and the world of physicality and the senses to the realm of meanings, higher creativity and subtler qualities – close to the soul. Love of beautiful objects is the prelude to love of beauty then follows love of the Source of beauty and other perfections.

It is essential for the seeker of self-knowledge to practice modesty, courage, wisdom and justice. When the lower self is groomed, and the natural, early vices of the ego have been checked and replaced with virtues, the new habits will drive the person towards higher attributes, which reside at the heart and are emitted by the soul. The ultimate religious, spiritual or moral grooming is to purify the heart so that the lights of the soul can shine through. When the lower self has been curbed and harnessed, the soul will simply reflect the essential qualities of generosity, mercy, forbearance, forgiveness, modesty, patience, knowledge and natural wholesomeness. When the vices of the ego yield to the virtues of the soul, a delightful unison and contentment takes place — sustainable Joy.

Adam's soul emerged from the Eternal Garden. Our struggle in this world is to turn away from all that is undesirable, gives false promises or unsustainable wholesomeness and return to the original abode of the safety of the soul and the Divine Presence. Through the discriminative capacity of the intellect, the self will submit to its soul and transmute to its original true love – Allah's

Universal Essence. This is the goal and the state of self-knowledge and enlightenment. Through grooming and restricting the ego, transcendence via soul consciousness to pure consciousness become the path of ascent back to the original state of bliss that is ever-present. The Qur'an describes the path of return to the perfect state. The hereafter is the final experiential theatre for the earthly possibilities of the return to the Garden of our spiritual origin.

## 4.1 Adam in Paradise

The human soul carries the imprints of paradise that existed before the so-called fall of Adam. Adam is the outcome of the Divine command that there will be a created being who can act as a vice-regent on earth. This new super-conscious being was at the pinnacle of a whole range of creations that evolved on earth. The angels were made to prostrate to Adam; their surprise and metaphorical objection was due to Adam's 'free will' and possible destructive tendency. The angels were not aware of Adam's inner constraints due to consciousness and the power of the soul within.

This earthly Adamic creation came about with his complementary pair — Eve. Adam in paradise had no needs but an inquisitiveness or transgression brought about a change in his paradisiacal state of blissfulness. The fall of Adam or his descent to earth was needed for the exposure to causalities, rationalities, other earthly creations and transient life.

Beside limited free will and self-awareness, Adam was given the knowledge of Divine attributes and qualities; his yearning for them made him restrained and self-correcting. Adam's soul carries the imprint of paradise and his offspring will always yearn for the garden of comfort and ease.

The rise of Adamic consciousness may be related to the evolvement and addition to the frontal cortex of the brain that enables the transcendental dimension of the human psyche. Before that, Adam was in paradise, the perfect garden where there were no needs, fears or the cycles of life and death. Paradise is devoid of time and space, as such it is a state of eternal bliss.

## 4.2 Descent and Ascent of Adam

The rise of the Adamic consciousness with its subtle challenges in the brain and mental processes, was accompanied by a sense of separation and inquisitiveness necessitated the descent to another domain and zone of experience, namely the earth. In this dynamic environment there are all kinds of dualities and new forces and factors that were non-existent before. This new cradle of mankind is based upon earthly trials, tests and struggles in order to move back towards the attainment of the state of peace and bliss as known by the soul before its imprisonment in the earthly realms.

It is on earth that evolution from the one cell towards the most complex human being took place. The physical nature of man is from earth, water, air and fire, whereas our spiritual essence is beyond our imagination. Every human being physically goes through a process of growing from a cell to a clot to a foetus, which matures within the womb and later outside of it for a few more months before stable growth occurs. The cycle of human creation begins with birth, then the subsequent evolvement of the self and its complexities, which present a great challenge with numerous mysteries due to the connection of behaviour and conduct with the subtle and non-discernible forces that bring them about. This is an amazing metaphor of how from Allah will emanate all kinds of creations, the pinnacle of which yearns to return back to the original state of perfection.

The cycles of birth and death are echoed in the descent of Adam and the ascent back to pure consciousness. The living emanates from the dead and the dead from the living and this paradox cannot be resolved rationally. It may dissolve through insight and illumination whose keys are faith in God and transcendence to truth.

## 4.3 Acting Stewardship

Adam and human species are composed of a sacred light or soul and a very complex material and energy structure. The physical person is made of an ever-growing and changing physical body activated through the brain and mind, whose source of energy is life emitted from the soul. Intrinsically, all human beings have the same basic makeup and have descended from one origin. The inner souls are like holograms reflecting the original Divine light and the essence of life.

Stewardship implies responsibility, knowledge, appropriate intentions and actions. Parents teach their offspring how best to conduct themselves as they grow towards adulthood. Every human being constantly connects with the outer world via the senses to maintain safety and wellbeing. Grown-up human beings who care for others and act as guardians and stewards will obviously have a higher sense of consciousness as expressed in love and altruism. Human attempts on earth are a way to replicate all the Divine qualities of mercy, generosity, forgiveness and other attributes that the soul knows to be great virtues emanating from God. The more successful the role of the steward, the closer he is to the Truth.

Self-responsibility, accountability, honesty, transparency and good intention are all necessary conditions to exercise this great privilege of vice-regency on earth. Reason, compassion and justice need to be matched by the highest sense of awareness and reference to the sacred light of the soul. The successful steward (man or woman) follows the revealed Prophetic way and remembrance of the Divine presence, aware that nothing ever escapes the knowledge of God. Whilst on earth, the responsible seeker reflects upon previous people who did not follow the Divine will and intention, and what the consequences of their actions were.

## 4.4 Human Composition

The souls or spirits of the children of Adam are a mysterious light package that is unique to human beings as it represents the ultimate Divine gift. The soul, which dwells within the heart is sacred, knows boundlessness and that which is eternal. The soul reproduces all of God's higher qualities and attributes, like a living hologram and emits these lights to the human mind whilst providing life and consciousness.

Creation on earth follows the laws of dualities and pluralities. Thus every human being is composed of the soul and its shadow companion — the self. The human self or ego is like the restless shadow of the soul and it desires all the qualities that reside within the soul. The real challenge to human beings is to recognise the connections between the lower self or ego and the higher self or soul, which occupies the *inner heart*, then groom the self.

The human evolvement is both biological as well as spiritual. When full maturity is reached, then priorities may begin to change towards seeking meaning in life and higher consciousness. Success in this endeavour relates to reforming and purifying the self, thereby accessing the heart and the soul therein. Thus, the mind becomes illumined with spiritual awakening.

The lower self is like a restless child that needs to be trained and groomed to accept boundaries and limitations. With ego restrictions come increased witnessing and insights. To see a situation with least emotional or mental bias, the light of the soul becomes a reference. Thus, the inner monitor is activated and thereby curbs the ego's impulsiveness and waywardness. The evolved being will realise that through faith and trust in God's presence in the heart, guidance and wellness will be the order. Then one can only be in constant gratitude for the great gift of the perfect soul and God's generosity.


## 4.5 Sublime and Ridiculous

Human beings can act more foolishly and destructively than any other animal. Equally, the offspring of Adam can be placed above angels for it is God and the angels that bless this creature. The lower self or ego wants to assert itself by achieving whatever it can imagine or desire, whilst it is the higher self or soul that basks in pure joy and perfections at all times. This inner conflict between a clown and a local king must be resolved before peace can ensue in the personal kingdom.

With wisdom and experience, a person is drawn more towards the lights, insights and openings that emanate from the soul within the heart. A youngster is more concerned with physical strength and mental agility, whereas the mature wise person enjoys prayers, meditation, inner peace, tranquillity and contentment. Without outer limitations and boundaries, the inner horizons of boundlessness will not appear – hence we need to strive towards incorporating the less of a clown, the more of a monarch.

Human life's experiences oscillates between good and bad, occasional happiness and much stress and difficulties. This oscillation will continue until the ego has submitted fully to its personal god or soul within the heart. With that submission comes greater benefits of trust and faith and the awareness at all times to act with good intentions and accountability. The lower self or ego has satanic qualities; all the vices such as deception, pretence and pride. The higher self relishes humbleness, compassion and service to others, and makes constant reference to God consciousness. Trickery can only bring its unexpected consequences upon the perpetrator.

The ego has to be laughed and mocked at, the soul loved, revered and followed. This is the way to resolve the paradox of human conflict; one part is false and foolish, the other is beautiful and sublime. All is from Allah.

## 4.6 Mind, Body and Soul

The uniqueness of human beings is clearly evident in our composition of a complex physical body and an intangible life force that is called soul or spirit, which is the essence of personal life force. We are a soul with a body. Our essence is constant and unchanging, yet we experience physical and mental changes and evolvement. The earth is our intermediate home where we learn to care for the body, harness our ego and emotions, yield to the soul and be content at heart. Our material structure is from the earth and our energy is from heavens. Thus, we straddle both domains.

Our biological organs, especially the five senses of hearing, seeing, feeling, smelling and tasting, as well as our inner senses of imagination and evaluation, help us to develop our mind, memory and personality. Each of our faculties has its metaphorical counterpart as far as the soul and higher consciousness is concerned. The Qur'an asserts that real blindness is not of the eye, but of the heart in the breast.

The most intricate entity in the body, self, soul make-up is that of the faculty of imagination, inner reflection, higher awareness and remembering. Ultimately, every human being is a sacred soul caught for a while within the microcosm of body and mind to resonate with the macrocosm. All quests of freedom and release from worldly limitations are instigated by the soul, which beams at the body through the mind and at its Master — Allah by its original covenant and sacred tie.

Without the evolving self and its ultimate will to yield in submission to its soul, there would be no possibility of a return to the consciousness of paradise and the eternal garden.

## 4.7 Author of Fate

Everything in existence is one of a pair; so are actions and reactions. Whatever begins, ends and every action has an equal and opposite reaction. As energies manifest in countless varieties from the most subtle to gross force, we cannot trace all the future implications of an intention or action. The laws of nature are so intricate that we can never predict the outcome of any action accurately, especially in relation to emotions.

This is why we often regret the outcome of many of our actions and thoughts. Collective actions make it more difficult to see how the reaction is in perfect balance with what was done by a group of people not on a path. Because the soul is universal, we tend to think that each one of us is at the centre of the universe and our biographies are special and unique. Thus, every human being tends to magnify the importance of events in their life and dramatise simple causalities of actions and reactions. The countless laws of nature can be understood mathematically or intellectually but will not be fully realised until experienced in actual life. Enlightenment implies spontaneous access to how everything is connected with everything else and that, in truth, an action and its outcome are inseparable. The timeless eternal truth is that there is only One original, sacred light and everything else overflows from that and returns back to its origin.

Only in the afterlife, this supreme truth becomes totally evident and clear. Then it will be seen that all that was considered good and bad in this life, and taken as challenges in the earthly nursery, were only to lead us to the truth of Oneness in action and essence. No action or reaction except by the One. Nothing in this creation escapes the fact that it is a closed system and that no energy or matter is ever created. When the physical veils of worldly existence are completely removed everything will be seen clearly as pure sacred light with nothing veiling that truth.

## 4.8 Punishment and Reward

Natural human inquisitiveness drives us towards knowledge of how things connect, relate and the hierarchy of causality. We seek independence and freedom to ensure the possibility of personal wellbeing and happiness.

The ultimate reward in life is sustained joyful contentment. There is no simple path to reach this state. Happiness comes about due to avoidance of misery, discordant thoughts and behaviour in life. Every person's problems and emotions differ from another as we create our own criteria of judgment, disappointment, blame, justified anger and so on.

God does not punish anyone. It is human beings, through their ignorance and inappropriate thoughts and actions, who produce an undesirable outcome that is labelled as punishment.

It is through good intentions and actions that we produce a better opportunity for wisdom and personal good will and helpfulness toward others. Good and selfless actions can override previous wrongdoings.

The faithful seeker can discern the relationship between one's inner state of wholesomeness or lack of it and the resultant outcome. It is God's design that through wrongdoings we will experience difficulties and complications — so that we correct our ways and be more accountable.

Ultimately doing good for others is to bring about goodness to one's self. In truth, there is no otherness — Allah is One.

## 4.9 Vices of the Self

The blissful state of Adam in the Garden was devoid of good or bad, for these complementary opposites and dualities belong to the earthly realm. A mature person knows what is a vice or undesirable deed as we tend to avoid or deny these tendencies. Vices mostly belong to the lower self and the basic survival mechanism before the rise of intellect, higher emotions and values.

It is natural for a young child to be disobedient, to occasionally lie and be deceptive. The list of these negative tendencies will cover a few pages but most commonly include extravagance, pride, indecency, wastefulness, love of wealth, arrogance, power and status and many other selfish traits. All of these tendencies belong to the lower self and can be checked or modified if there is a reflection from the soul or the higher self. When one becomes aware of the opposite virtues, these natural, but undesirable tendencies may then lead to good ethical behaviour.

In the moment of anger or impatience, a flash of reflection regarding the futility or inappropriateness of such a behaviour can redress the emotional imbalance. It can even lead to the wisdom of patience and helpful behaviour. The lower self is endowed with countless vices that make one suffer unless one practices awareness and application of the virtues that are opposite to the vices. Wrongful expectation could lead to compassion and patience. Fear could lead to courage. Loss of trust and faith in God could lead to asking for forgiveness and the determination to remain on the path of virtue and constant remembrance of the Divine presence and perfection. The lower self is merely a veil over the soul, like the husk or shell over a kernel — it needs to crack before we attain the goodness inside.

## 4.10 Virtues of the Soul

Through faithful good actions, prayers and meditation, we realise the sacred presence of the soul within ourselves. Wisdom will show us that vices belong to the ego and are natural for early evolution, whilst recognition of virtues is part of spiritual growth and evolvement.

Normally we would like to appear to be charitable, patient, forgiving and willing to sacrifice for others' sake – and then to have our desirable qualities acknowledged as good by others. Religious-minded people would like to appear as pious, spiritually mature, and even perfect. The wish and desire to be seen as virtuous and good does not necessarily mean that those qualities are predominant and real.

Praising God means love and praise of Allah's numerous attributes and qualities that we aspire towards during our life. The human soul has been imprinted in a mysterious sense with all of the Divine virtues of love, compassion, selflessness, generosity, forgiveness, courage, patience and others. It is the restless lower self that is endowed with vices that it denies, for it wants to emulate the perfection of the soul. This is why, if these vices are not reformed, the ego becomes a master of hypocrisy and deception.

The lower self needs to be groomed to learn to submit and trust in its transformation and unification with its soul. This step is the beginning of spiritual awakening and unison between heart and mind.

The remedies are religious practices, especially remembrance of death and the hereafter. To act against the lower tendencies and declare one's faults and ignorance will help to transcend the ego and begin to enjoy the virtues and perfection of the soul.

## 4.11 The Wholesome Heart

The physical heart is a major organ of the human body. The metaphorical heart is where the soul inhabits and emits its life force. It is this heart that is often referred to as the most important element in spiritual progress. There can be numerous diseases of this heart, which range from being sick, jealous, mean and tarnished to being overly attached, as well as numerous other ailments. Our mind is the connecting point between the inner and the outer world enabling us to maintain a balanced life. The metaphorical or inner heart needs to be purified so that the connection becomes clear between the earthly world and the sacred soul within this heart.

Generally, it is easier to restrict the ego and the lower self through improved behaviour, and accountability. To purify the heart and render it wholesome, the inner heart requires different disciplines and tutelage than the mind and conduct. Human love for meditation, peace or even monastic life is a sign that we want to purify the heart from all outer tarnishes. A purified heart has no lust, anger or attachments within it, therefore the light of God will shine through it. The ultimate test is the willingness to give away whatever one loves to keep.

When the heart is pure, the soul will bring about the realisation that life is ever-perfect and eternal. The truly awakened heart has no concern about personal death, for it knows that the soul is eternal. Respect for life on earth can be genuine due to the realisation of the sacredness of the soul within the heart. Through reverence of the soul, we also tolerate or respect other human aspects.

It is the wholesome heart that enables us to pick up signals from the unseen, past, present or future and endows us with intuitive, spontaneous insights. The purified heart allows the light of the soul to shine through whatever Allah wills in His infinite generosity.

## 4.12 To Witness and Transcend

Self-awareness and clear witnessing are qualities of the heart. To achieve these qualities, one needs to train and discipline one's mind and intellect. To witness a situation properly, the veils of self-judgment, expectations, past memory and other ego considerations need to be eliminated. One needs to be disengaged from involvement in that situation. This neutral stance is a function of the inner heart. It is sometimes referred to as objective evaluation, although the subject and object do always have some connection. Through our senses, we respond or react but by reference to past experiences and to the higher state of the soul, we can then put matters into perspective.

All aspects of self-reformation and spiritual evolvement imply less rash and emotional or egotistic tendencies and more orientation towards listening and responding to the heart and the light of the soul within it.

The impulse of self-preservation is within all of us and reacts to the slightest danger to the body, mind and self image or ego. Through the light of the inner witnessor, the monitor force interferes to bring about the higher influence of the soul.

It is only then that we can escape the tyranny of being caught in the opposing forces of the lower self and the higher self. Adam fell through the hole of self-concern and can only climb back through the ladder of soul consciousness and God's mercy.

## 4.13 Decree and Destiny

Whatever is in existence is according to a measure and follows causality and patterns of quality and quantity. Due to the interaction between countless entities and systems, we fail to see the simplicity of natural laws. God has decreed that the universe follows laws that can be discerned by us as physical, mathematical, chemical, and electromagnetic terms, and through other types of knowledge. From the subtlest sacred light of the unseen emerge the most solid metals. No matter what there is in creation, it is subject to decrees and laws. We are shown so many of these natural laws, as encouragement for us to accept by faith and trust.

Destiny is a personal experience that is the result of our intentions and actions interacting with the natural laws that govern existence. Everyone desires perfect destiny, yet most of us experience difficult, challenging and undesirable ends. Human beings, however, have the will to change intentions, attitudes and directions in their life. It is the most wonderful gift to be able to experience a positive outcome as a result of good and appropriate actions. We are programmed to realise goodness. God is ever-perfect.

A good-natured human being with a sincere willingness to serve others selflessly will experience grace and generosity that transcends logic and common sense. Good destiny is a result of good behaviour, good expectation, good thoughts and perseverance in all that is virtuous and good. Equally, the reverse is true when one is subjecting oneself to decrees and laws that are disruptive and destructive.

It is only the human being who has this choice and freewill to follow the lower tendencies and suffer or to diligently seek the light of the soul. Decrees and laws do not change but we experience dramatic change in outcome according to our intention and choices.

## 4.14 The Complete Person

Adam and Eve complement each other in paradise and on earth. This is both a physical reality and a metaphor of how two entities emanate from one source and return back to the same unity.
All human beings have a sacred spirit or soul blown into them

and their ultimate purpose in life is to realise and submit to this great gift, this light.

A baby begins life mostly concerned with senses and physical gratification. A wise person will be more concerned about meanings in life, insights, subtle knowledge and intuitions. We emerge from the unseen into the world of material causalities, which veil the unseen and the potential inner ease and joy due to earthly uncertainties.

A good life can be achieved when the individual is aware of their intentions and accepts responsibility and accountability at all times. A mature person submits to the fact that human needs and desires are endless. Submission, or Islam, is the first step to a good life, then comes living faith and trust in God's Perfect Mercy and Justice, irrespective of circumstances. Then one can bask in the security and knowledge of Divine guidance through one's own soul.

All prophets and messengers have perfected their journeys and attained the purpose of life, which is to witness the light of Allah and live according to it. We may deny religion or faith but we cannot deny the fact that there were beings who lived this life in a manner that is an example to whoever is striding towards a better understanding of life. With living faith and trust, the faithful seeker will also realise the infinite mercy and grace of God, and with that exposure and realisation, the enlightened person can only be in ecstatic gratitude. This is the complete person.

## 4.15 Full Consciousness

Consciousness operates at many levels and spheres. Over millennia of years, the cell has evolved to complex systems with intricate physics and chemistry activated by subtler forces, all of which emanate from light and the original life force. The companion of light is consciousness and all of its qualities, and, thus, consciousness is the vast field due to which life emerges. The fish in the sea take the water for granted; all conscious creatures too, take consciousness for granted and, thus, we can never resolve and define the nature of consciousness but can discern different levels, qualities and states of it.

All levels of consciousness emanate from One Supreme or pure consciousness. A human being begins life by experiencing and developing personal, conditioned or local consciousness – and then through interaction with others, we expand personal consciousness vertically and horizontally. Biological evolution is taken for granted but spiritual evolvement requires proper intention, willpower and serious application. As we grow in wisdom, knowledge and insights, we find that this ocean of consciousness in which life thrives is endless and that the human conditioned consciousness could only grow within the limitations of space and time.

A mature and evolved seeker desires to go beyond the limitations of space and time and that desire is in response to the pervading pure consciousness that is feeding the personal consciousness. Full consciousness is the desired destiny for all human beings. Adam fell from the Garden due to self-consciousness and the climb back is through the ladder of the higher self and pure consciousness — as was his original state in paradise. God consciousness includes earthly and all other lower consciousnesses that have emanated from it. The one original light prevails upon every other light and shadow. Allah is the light of heavens and earth.

## Chapter 5

## Earthly Life and the Hereafter

Introduction
5.1　Transient Living
5.2　Forms and Meanings
5.3　Veils and Deceptions
5.4　Elusive Security
5.5　Faithless Worldliness
5.6　Faith and Righteousness
5.7　Perfections of Afflictions
5.8　For Others' Sake?
5.9　Cleverness and Wisdom
5.10　War and Peace
5.11　Durable Justice
5.12　Failure, Success and Victory
5.13　Hell and Paradise
5.14　Wholesome Life
5.15　Death and the Hereafter
5.16　Universal Resurrection
5.17　Perfection of Destiny

# 5

# Earthly Life and the Hereafter

**Introduction**

Allah created the confinement and limitations of time and space as an earthly nursery for the family of Adam to bridge the gap between earthly and heavenly states through personal will and spiritual evolvement. All aspects of life are experienced as part of the dynamics of cause and effect, which criss-cross and re-emerge from each other. Today is yesterday's child and the mother of tomorrow. The entire creation is caught in the web of interlinks and numerous levels of influences and relationships; spheres within spheres strung along time and space.

The early biological growth of a human being is a prelude to spiritual evolvement and realisation of the One source of life behind multiplicity and dualities. Family, clans and culture are necessary for the early evolvement of human beings and provide the basis upon which our senses and experiences mature towards higher consciousness. Consciousness of individuality and survival is a necessary foundation for transcendence and arrival.

A society is an aggregate of individuals interacting and influencing each other within cultural norms and customs. The styles, habits and material aspects of a culture are naturally influenced by its history, geography, environment and other socio-economic factors. The state of a people is a function of many complex exogenous and endogenous influences. The rise and fall of nations and people is highly dependent on the presence or absence of durable social qualities such as good ethics, morality, justice and community conscience. The most important quality in human leadership is the recognition and presence of the Prophetic or spiritual reference, which reflects Divine justice and human accountability to strive towards at all times.

Human life is measured according to material, physical, mental and spiritual qualities. Values of modesty, humility, generosity, tolerance, and patience, as well as other virtues, are indispensable for sustainable wellbeing and general contentment. Arrogance, corruption, frivolous pleasure and luxury, wastefulness and lack of care for others are all signs for weakness in the community and cause for its possible breakdown. The affliction that befalls people is often due to the wrong actions of a section of that society, resulting in the disintegration of the whole. Wise leadership cannot impose values that the people are not ready to adopt wholeheartedly whether rational or religious. The Qur'an declares that religion cannot be forced upon people.

The Qur'an encourages people to travel across the earth and reflect upon the various great ancient civilisations, which collapsed then vanished. It also relates situations that illustrate examples of decent people seeking knowledge of the Divine, who were graced with goodness following a spiritual path. The Prophet Solomon and his people are such an example. Due to his knowledge, sincere submission and perfection of his worship, Solomon had access to the powers of the invisible realm, such as *Jinn* and other supernatural forces. He was rewarded with the mastery of both the outer and the inner worlds.

In the same way individuals grow, develop, succeed, weaken, decline and then die, nations, too, follow the same type of pattern but on a different timescale and level of predictability. A society or a nation is as strong as the quality of its individual members and their wise leadership.

Wise and just leadership with moral commitment and wholesome religious or spiritual aspirations are an important factor in a society's quality of life.

The natural cyclical occurrence of life and death on earth is one of the cornerstones of prophetic teachings. The Qur'an brings this creational issue to the fore. Indeed, Islam is built on the foundation of God-awareness, accountability at all times and constant reference to the hereafter. In terms of human conduct and self-awareness, remembrance of death and virtuous actions are essential factors in spiritual awakening.

Allah describes the condition and experience of the Hereafter as based on the individual's earthly actions and intentions. Each person will relive what was earned in this life. Paradise and hell are the two extreme states or destinies that will be experienced as a consequence of the worldly journey. Aspects of hell and paradise are often experienced on earth to a limited extent by most of us. Those who perpetuate injustice, brutality and tyranny without accountability will be requited for their wrongdoing in the next life. Those who have lived in piety and service, maintaining peace and goodwill for all will enter the abode of permanent bliss in the garden of the Hereafter.

This world, caught in time and space, is the realm of relative experiences that leads to a boundless phase beyond it. Adam was created in the Garden but needed to be exposed to the dark side of the equation and earthly struggles to exercise will and desire for salvation and liberation from exile. His children have to earn their return to that Garden through intelligent submission, dedicated action and good expectations of Allah's generosity.

The relative pleasures and afflictions of this world are only small samples of the everlasting experience of the Hereafter.

Thus, there are many minor hells and gardens in this world that teach us discrimination and wisdom in preparation for the next abode. If we realise the One Divine Light behind all light and shadows in this world, then after departure from this earthly body that sacred knowledge will deliver us to the appropriate new phase of heavenly life.

## 5.1 Transient Living

Human life on earth is limited and will end, whereas life is eternal, as is its essence — Allah. Adam's soul is imprinted with that knowledge. Thus every person is driven to a better destiny and wholesome life on earth and hereafter.

All of our experiences here are within time and space, thus everything has a beginning and an end. Everything in our life is transient and subject to change and dualities, some of which are constructive and attractive whilst others are undesirable and destructive. Life on earth is a constant struggle in order to bring about what is considered good and durable and to repulse that which is considered bad or difficult. We truly love stability, although deep down we know that it is unattainable on earth. Yet still, the futile outer search continues for better secure situations.

With spiritual maturity, we can come to terms with outer transience as experienced in body and mind and discover constancy at heart. Permanent life is beyond earthly experience and death is the entry point. As for the quality of that life, it is dependent on the extent of our spiritual awakening in this life and realisation of Allah's Lordship and perfections.

All life on earth is an intermediate stage between the eternal source of life before creation, the material and physical realities and identifications on earth. Every self leaves this world when the power of the soul departs to another realm carrying with it the residues of personality and the extent of its surrender and faith to its Creator. The urgency of this life manifests in that the lower nature of the human being can never be content or satisfied, whilst the soul is ever-secure. Our purpose is to unify self and soul and coast along towards the inevitable destiny.

## 5.2 Forms and Meanings

When Adam became self-conscious and felt his separate identity, there arose the perpetual quest to return to the bliss of the Garden of Unity. The human form is meant to search for meaning, purpose and transcendence.

In paradise, there was no awareness or consciousness beyond the primal states of sacred unity. The distracting tree implies a separation between forms and their meanings and the advent of duality. Anything that has an outer shape or form has an inner energy pattern that is its subtle root or origin. The primary impulse of vegetation is to spread out on earth exalting the Divine attribute of vastness and prevalence. This process is carried out physically by producing attractive fruits that birds and other animals can eat and, spread the seeds elsewhere. Other plants use wind power and fly their seeds across. All of these methods share the same purpose or meaning of spreading and increasing. All other desirable attributes emanate from the same source and connect in their origin to the One essence. This is how the inner and outer domains are connected and yet, appear separate within space and time.

We desire strong houses and secure food supplies, yet in truth our abode on earth is as flimsy as a spiderweb. The meaning of this desire lies in our soul, which is ever-secure and eternal. We are often hasty, and the real purpose of impatience is for the lower self to surrender to its soul and be at peace. Original language developed from these multitudes of expressive forms attempting to convey a meaning. If we don't say what we mean or act upon what we say, then we are increasing the veils of the lower self that may distort the light of the soul. An evolved human being is he or she who does not try to deceive by camouflaged or falsified language. The human challenge on earth is to see unity in diversity and that includes connection between energy and matter at every level of creation.

## 5.3 Veils and Deceptions

Total clarity is seen through the lenses of Oneness with no interference of otherness. For reason and discrimination to arise, we need relative situations where Truth or Reality is shaded or veiled. Otherwise, the full light of Oneness will overcome all secondary realities and existences.

The lower self and its biological evolution is a cover upon the higher self and its truth. The lower self or ego is a necessary condition for growth initially. A child grows into the teens asserting its separate identity and individuality; at maturity an intelligent person realises that essentially we are all the same in our desires, endeavours, independencies and insecurities, although outer actions and directions seem different.

The seed of a tree is often covered and will sprout after the decay of the outer shell. The lower self or the ego is like the outer shell, whose purpose is early protection to allow for survival; and maturity of the body and its mind before the advent of spiritual growth. The pampered ego can use all kinds of deceptions, justifications and self-entitlement to strengthen and prolong the elusive reality of its identity. It is a mad, thirsty person lost in the desert, chasing mirages. Even when one has arrived at the non-existent water shore, the self will invent another mirage as an excuse or apportion blame to maintain its image. Only when the self begins to admit its inadequacy and dependence upon its soul – which is the gift of God of grace, mercy and generosity, can the process of disappearance of veils and covers upon the soul begin.

The hereafter clearly reveals the extent of self-delusions and deceptions, for in that state all veils are fully removed and the concept of time and space becomes a thin memory of a misty past. In the hereafter, we may recall years on earth as instances — the veils are removed and truth is effulgent.

## 5.4 Elusive Security

Before the rise of self-awareness and separate personal identity, there was no notion of security. In this world, we relentlessly pursue outer security that can never be adequate without inner certainty and God consciousness. We need to do our best but always need to refer to Allah as the ultimate source of reliance and trust.

As the self grows and the mind develops, a normal human being seeks a state of reliability and goodness that is constant. The soul is ever-content and joyful and the self desires to attain that state. Everyone hopes that their inner state will be better in future. The early impulse for every individual is outer security for survival, strength and durability. The need for shelter, food and other human beings to support one is primal and remains so throughout one's life. It is through higher consciousness that we realise that we are only fully secure to the extent of our God consciousness. God is eternal and ever-lasting and the soul within the heart is ever-secure and content in its knowledge of God and His will. Spiritual progress implies the surrender of the self with all its quests and desires to the soul.

Outer material securities are necessary up to a point and we need to pursue these according to personal needs. The danger, of course, is that we get carried away with love of possessions and power to control. Only the wise realise that there is a limit to outer security and that the purpose of this drive is to rely more and more upon the inner light within the heart and live in faith and knowledge of God's mastery and guidance. Outer security is ever-elusive; it is a good start if it leads to inner reliance and the joyful knowledge that everything is created to perfect design and is sustained by Him. Otherwise, the relentless quest for security and wealth will lead to disappointment in this life and the hereafter.

## 5.5 Faithless Worldliness

The only hope for Adam's offspring on earth is to develop faith and trust in the realisation of Oneness and its grace that envelops the universe, without denying the conditioned experience of otherness. Otherwise, total worldly immersion is like a dark dungeon that can only bring about ultimate suffocation and desperation.

Many individuals and societies are obsessed with trying to perfect the outer existential circumstances in the hope of bringing about sustainable happiness. The mind and the lower self can be the ultimate veils of progress in God consciousness. A person who relies entirely upon one's own independent actions will be more trapped in the illusion of separation from God consciousness and the Oneness that engulfs the universe. Causality and hard rationality can veil life's wide horizons as it provides justifications for not looking beyond the limitations of time and space and lower consciousness.

The restless lower self is a natural shadow of the soul and reflects and echoes millions of years of survival, instinct and biological evolution. The soul is not affected by space-time whilst the self carries memories and imprints of the past. The more we refer to the higher intellect and the light within the heart which relates to the frontal cortex, the more likely it is that we begin to see on the horizon our Adamic origin before descent to earth and confinement in space and time. There are those who excel in this world to such an extent that there will be only be shock and alienation for them in the hereafter. The love of power, control, status and other attractions in this world sap all the energy that could make us look at the horizon beyond this world. Most humans get caught in this darkness. If we deny the hereafter, then there can only be hardship (for futile struggle) in this world and the next (described as fire of purification). What is needed is not denial or renunciation of this world, but living it lightly with as small a footprint as one stepping stone to the next. To live on earth without faith and trust in a perfect outcome is to deny the presence of God's generosity, grace and the purpose of creation.

## 5.6 Faith and Righteousness

A faithful seeker recognises the transience of this world and continues to seek sustainable wellbeing through prayers and God consciousness. Selfishness is natural for the lower self, while generosity is the nature of the soul. Application of religion will lead to a practical faith with appropriate intentions and actions that reduce egotistic tendencies and excessive self-concern. Righteous actions imply any action that brings the individual closer to the liberating light of the heart rather than the restrictive logic of mind and ego.

The quiet, intelligent person desires a state of wellbeing that it is not entirely dependent upon the material and physical. All actions are within dualities and will leave some side-effect upon us. Thus, every person is the outcome of their past intentions and actions and the subtle hopes and desires behind them. Intentions, actions and outcome will lead the reflective person to the point of constant reference to God consciousness before undertaking worldly actions to reduce the burden of personal biography and the burdens of the past.

Simple trust and faith in the hereafter can refine our intentions and actions because they connect the immediate awareness and local consciousness with pure consciousness. Faith may begin blindly but can end up with pure light that leads one to do the appropriate 'pure' actions, at the right time and at the right place. The ultimate righteous action is described as entirely for God's sake with no expectations for worldly reward. Yet, righteous action does not imply denial of this world, for life on earth is a prelude and a preparation for eternal life upon the departure of the soul from its worldly abode. Whoever lives in this world with constant reference to the hereafter and acts appropriately will experience Divine grace and the state of the garden in this life (temporarily) and the hereafter in timelessness.

## 5.7 Perfections of Afflictions

The descent of Adam carries with it the promise and prescription for the ascent. God's mercy and generosity is endless and can be experienced in every situation if we perceive and witness with insight and reflection on the perfection of the whole scene and events.

There is no time that a person is without any needs, desires or aspirations. The curiosity of Adam about the tree implies the constant search, inquisitiveness and yearning for knowledge of all. Struggles, afflictions and difficulties are constant companions of the human journey on earth and this state increases in intensity with increased spirituality. It appears darkest just before dawn.

Human life and experience is balanced between dualities, and all outer afflictions are balanced by inner purification and correction in direction and purpose. For the spiritual seeker, outer difficulties are the key to inner ease and insight. Through God consciousness, one develops a lessened concern regarding worldly difficulties and afflictions. It is what will push us towards the ever-present grace and Divine offering.

The entire universe is in a state of unity but appears to drift apart with countless entities all of which will return back to the original unity after a few billion years. The human being can realise the ever-present state by reference to the sacred soul within the purified heart.

It is by needs and difficulties that God draws us closer to the light of God consciousness if we surrender, have faith and realise Divine perfection. Allah's theatre includes all heavens and earth.

The intelligent and wise seeker will restrict distracting tendencies and will realise the immense richness and generosity of the Creator. Outer difficulties can be a great drive towards inner ease and contentment. Then, one is living in the moment fully and thereby, realising the sacred presence beyond all limitations.

## 5.8 For Others' Sake?

God is the only true Reality and all other realities emanate and return to the One Real. Thus, whatever good is done will increase knowledge of God's ways and it is, therefore, for one's own sake. God doesn't need our prayers or good actions; we need these to save ourselves from the lower self.

When biological maturity is attained, the self may begin to question the meaning and purpose of life and the wise person will realise, the sameness of other people's endeavours and hopes. Outwardly, there are no two people or instances that are the same, whereas inwardly we all desire contentment, equilibrium, wellbeing and happiness. If we look at our outer manifestations, whether it is the shape of a body, the colour of a skin or other features of personality, we only find differentiation and otherness. By looking inwardly to the hearts and the essence of our life (namely the soul), we find similarity and Oneness. With sight, we see differences, and with insight, we see similarities. Thus for the sake of others is an excuse to be less egocentric and thereby drawn towards the higher self.

When a wise person realises that the main barrier to God consciousness is the restless lower self, the only question that remains is how to overcome this obstacle. Serving those nearest, such as parents, neighbours, community and humanity at large are amongst the most effective remedies. Therefore, we begin by assuming that we are helping others and serving humanity or mankind for God's sake. An enlightened being knows that there is only One sake (the universal soul) and our earthly struggles are to do with returning the shadowy self to its magical fountain and origin, the soul at heart. In truth, there is only Oneness. Allah is the One and only One and it is the ultimate intelligence to realise this truth and live by it — truly happy.

## 5.9 Cleverness and Wisdom

God warns us against deceptions, falsehood, lies and hypocrisy. To be honest, upright and ready to ask forgiveness of God is necessary for spiritual development.

The human mind and brain can be used in distorted ways that produce a confused behaviour and outlook on life. Human development begins with differentiation and self-identification. Maturity and grooming of the lower self, together with wisdom, religious and spiritual practices, can lead to higher awareness of the Divine presence and the purposefulness and direction of life.

Strict ethical practices and caution protect against the subtle ways the lower self can impede spiritual growth. The self, ego and mind can play tricks and use all kinds of justifications to enhance the ego and its assumption of virtues and higher qualities. The lower self is easily deceived by Satan to assert its false identity and independence of the light of the soul within the heart. It is self-deception and delusions that block natural progress towards higher awareness.

The same mind that is often the centre of deception and cleverness to justify egotistic distractions can be sublimated to higher intellect, insights and openings to the lights of the heart. The self can be both destructive as well as the key to higher spiritual evolvement.

It is easier for simple folk, who are often considered by worldly measures as weak and ineffectual, to live in fidelity to their heart's inner soul voice. Total honesty and courage are essential foundations to wisdom and real justice. The purified heart enables the light of the soul to shine across the spectrum of human consciousness enabling the individual to refer their intentions, actions and thoughts to the perfect light of truth and thereby ascending to spiritual wisdom.

## 5.10 War and Peace

Within every person lie the two aspects of the self; the lower ego and the higher soul. Thus, inner conflict is natural and this challenge will only come to an end when the divided self and the apparent separation between conditioned consciousness (ego) and higher consciousness (soul) has ended in their unity.

This inner conflict reflects the metaphor of the tree that caused Adam to descend to earth — Oneness that can only be realised by transcending two-ness. Without affliction and discord, we will not fully appreciate peace and harmony.

Peace and lasting tranquillity within an individual can radiate to others and produce a calming effect. Equally, a confused and angry person can also affect others adversely. The quality of a group of people is clearly affected by the state of its leading members.

For an individual to be guided by God consciousness, faith and good actions are necessary conditions. Struggle in the way of goodness, justice, and peace is part of the duties of a Muslim. So is migration to avoid corruption and suffering. War in self-defence is also sometimes unavoidable, although Allah enjoins peace and goodwill amongst all people.

Human injustice on earth makes everyone suffer and as we have an innate tendency towards goodness and wellbeing for all, it is a natural evolutionary inclination for all of humanity to resent injustice and abusiveness.

It is quite natural for a child to be self-absorbed and aggressive. This impulse relates to some and is deeply engrained within us. With growth in consciousness, we realise that all such lower tendencies are detrimental to spiritual growth and lasting wellbeing. When a seeker is established in self-knowledge and God consciousness, then he has transcended all inner battles and conflicts. The enlightened person basks in the state of utter contentment in harmony with all creation.

## 5.11 Durable Justice

To attain stable goodness on earth is one of the main challenges in human life. Good and bad, life and death, health and illness constantly interact and interchange their positions. The middle path means understanding both extremes and maintaining a balanced middle position. Our essential make-up is earthly and changeable, heavenly and eternal — body and soul.

Justice is the maintenance of balance between creational dualities and multiplicities of forces in creation. It is only through just actions that any situation can be maintained or prolonged; any natural system disturbed by us can be said to be out of balance.

It is incumbent upon us human beings to know what the optimum balance is and to try not to disturb it, whether in relation to our own sake, for society or the environment. Losing this balance can be a cause of destruction of earthly life. Nature has its own natural boundaries that are in actual fact corrective measures to maintain the earth's destiny.

On earth, all of us wish to experience justice at all levels, yet all human justice is relative and temporary. Only by reference to the absolute justice of God can our practices on earth be more durable. By faith in God's mercy and guidance, by constant watchfulness of the egotistic pitfalls and willingness to admit mistakes, we will improve our hope for durable justice at all levels.

The enlightened person knows that we all live in a transient and relative world and that nothing can ever be fixed or preserved in this dynamic flux. Yet, no person striving towards wholesomeness can deny the urge to witnessing perfection or bringing about durable justice to all. We all seek stability, constancy and total security and yet we know none of these are attainable within the dynamics of space and time. Durable justice is written in the wholesome heart and engrained in the human soul.

## 5.12 Failure, Success and Victory

Lasting victory belongs to Allah and every human endeavour is as good as the extent to which it is aligned with Allah's ways and will. Most human endeavours in this life are to enable a desire or need to be satisfied or fulfilled.

Success generally means momentary contentment due to an achievement of a goal at the end of struggle. Failure is missing a target or an opportunity. Common ideas regarding success or failure are part of natural life on earth for everyone. Victory, however, implies a greater measure of durable success. When it relates to wellbeing or happiness, victory can only be achieved if our reference is higher consciousness and not local or transient awareness.

Sustained victory is only by Allah. If one's worldly actions are meant to improve other people's wellbeing and, ultimately, grant greater access to God consciousness, then irrespective of visible outcome, the actor will be at the door to inner victory.

To follow one's heart truly is to follow the light of the soul within the heart. To follow the prophetic path and the sacred light is to be on the highway towards true victory, thus even those who have died in the just cause are considered ever-living beings and martyrs in the way of truth. Worldly success and failure are states that lead the faithful seeker eventually to witness Allah's victory in all situations.

The wise person realises that the most important business in this life is to access higher consciousness and refer to it by remembering that whatever is on earth is there in order to perfect its adoration and worship of Allah. Thus, victory is realised through transformative worship.

## 5.13 Hell and Paradise

Hell and Paradise are real substitute states that are experienced by human beings on earth to varying degrees of intensity and duration. Then there is the Hell and Paradise of the hereafter — eternal.

For someone who creates constant turmoil, misery and agitation on earth, the burning fire of the hereafter is a just destination. Equally, if a person has faith, sincerity, cares for other humans and performs wise actions, he or she will witness God's generosity and grace at all times; for them then the abode of paradise in the hereafter is a natural conclusion.

Adam was created in the garden of paradise without self-awareness or discrimination between wisdom and folly. The children of Adam on earth can choose and exercise their will to realise different personal destinies. A wise person on earth sees the states of hell and paradise all around and is always cautious of the slippery path of hell. The enticing energy of Satan allures the lower self towards distractions and short-lived pleasures that ultimately often lead to difficulties and regrets.

The path of paradise is difficult to begin with, for it requires diligent, responsible action, with constant reference to higher consciousness and accountability. When the ego is subdued and the heart purified, one begins the joy of living by the will of God as it is emitted by the soul within the heart.

The states that are described in the hereafter would have been already experienced on earth in the form of hell or paradise. The children of Adam are indeed stewards on earth and our life here is to practice, rehearse and be ready to return to the original garden or hell.

## 5.14 Wholesome Life

We are heavenly souls transiting through earth back to heaven. Human life on earth begins with the development of outer and inner senses, then the faculties of imagination, reflection, thinking and higher intellect. Initially, a child needs to be helped, protected and guided.

The Lord of the universe has endowed parents with demi-lordship for their children. With maturity, greater self-awareness, acceptance of responsibility and inner guidance, the new person can take over.

The gift of life and the treasure of the soul are glorious and sacred and must be treated with caution, reverence and love. The mature seeker looks for meanings in events and is confident in God's guidance, mercy and forgiveness. A wholesome life implies living fully in the world of dualities and their challenges by constant reference to the soul that brings about constancy and stability along the journey.

A person's life is wholesome and healthy when everything in creation is seen as an example of the Creator's perfection. An awakened seeker of truth is in constant reference to the voice and signals of the heart whilst responding to outer stimuli and events. An enlightened person's heart is pure from all attachments and anxieties, for it is illumined by the sacred effulgence of the soul.

Inner freedom is the real indicator of wholesome living. A wholesome life is the unification of body, mind, heart and soul due to constant reference to the unifying light of God. This life is given by Allah, sustained by Him and returns to Him — there is no God but the one and only God.

## 5.15 Death and the Hereafter

Adam descended to earth to be challenged by all the limitations and necessary interactions, connectedness and yearning to return to the bliss of paradise. After death, we experience the hereafter. To begin with, the consciousness of a deceased person still has some notion of space and time but after a while, the soul with its shadow companion — the earthly ego — carries on to a new realm beyond our imagination. All of our human experiences on earth are limited by the speed of light and the hereafter is beyond that. There may well be some deep subconscious memory of the original paradise, but more than that the soul will carry with it the effects of earthly exposure, actions and spiritual evolvement.

It is in the hereafter that every self will fully experience and realise the effects of its intentions and actions on earth, down to the details even of the smallest events. Permanent hell or paradise as referred to in the afterlife mean that durations in that realm are totally different to early times. If one's life on earth had helped to exercise God consciousness and the person left this world with illuminated faith and contentment, then the passage through resurrection will happen with ease. Otherwise, processes of purification (chastisements) will be experienced before the soul carries along its final journey. Every soul will be given its just due in the hereafter.

Immediately after death, there is a twilight zone, where the soul-self energy entity undergoes adjustments due to the loss of the body, mind and will to act. It is during this intermediate state that the deceased experiences bewilderment and loss. Eventually the two major events of universal death and resurrection will take place on the Day of Reckoning.

## 5.16 Universal Resurrection

Whatever is born will die. Individual entities and creations, as well as celestial bodies and galaxies, all have beginnings and ends. Whatever is on this earth has its roots in the heavens. Every entity that is within the limitations of space and time has its essence beyond the boundaries of any place or time.

Death is the end of what appeared on earth and resurrection is the return to origin, with an earthly colour or tag representing our deeds and state of evolvement in consciousness. Whatever has emanated from heavens onto earth will also return to heavens with an additional earthly biography and colours superimposed upon the original purity.

Human experiences on this earth are preludes and preparations to the witnessing and experiencing of the amazing truth that is beyond human capacity or grasp and will be fully realised after death and upon resurrection.

Life on earth has occurred over millennia and was subject to evolutionary growth, whereas resurrection will be instantaneous. All creations exist within the womb of space and time; resurrection is beyond those limits and ideas. It is a great mystery that awaits us all.

The universe began at one instant, a few billions of years ago, and will also probably end after a few billions of years from now. The universe will end in a major collapse and after this total death there will be a total rise to witness Truth in the Divine Presence. Total death followed by total re-emergence for every soul to be recomposed according to its deeds on earth.

## 5.17 Perfection of Destiny

Everything belongs to Allah and will return to Him. Human beings return with the outcome of their deeds on earth tied to them. Quality of life on earth and after death is marked by the quality of the purity of their heart, intentions and actions. The extent of God consciousness will determine our destiny at all times.

Every moment has a destiny but we only take notice when an event comes to an end or a shock brings about success or failure. Every day ends up with its destiny at nightfall and every life reaches its destiny at the point of death.

For believers as well as those who have no interest in higher consciousness, there is a desire for a good or happy destiny. In all of our endeavours on earth, our projects, travels and human relationships, we hope for an increased state of contentment and happiness, thereby achieving a better destiny.

Human hope drives us towards improving our intentions and actions so that irrespective of outer events or situations we can reach a better destiny. Perfect destiny is to do with constant contentment and happiness. Even though this state may be elusive to most of us on earth, no one can stop desiring it or striving for it. God consciousness and the presence of the Lord of creation is the ultimate destiny.

God, who has created all, permeated all that is known and unknown and thereby governs all that exists – from inception and towards its perfect destiny – return to source. To realise Divine perfection and the glorious attributes and qualities that are emitted as an overflow from the One essence is the path to realise perfect destiny — always.

**Chapter 6**

**Prophets of Islam**

Introduction
6.1  Many Prophets with One Message
6.2  Different Cultures and People
6.3  Prophetic Qualities
6.4  Courage and Sacrifice of Prophets
6.5  Living Islam
6.6  Equity, Charity and Justice
6.7  Laws and Boundaries
6.8  Religious Rituals and Practices
6.9  Relationships, Duties and Courtesies
6.10  Perfect Worship
6.11  The Way of Muhammad
6.12  Humanity and Divinity
6.13  Universal Mercy and Grace

# 6

# Prophets of Islam

**Introduction**

A prophet is a normal human being who is intensely connected to the ultimate reference point and source of guidance: Allah. A prophet's inner state is especially ready to receive sacred revelations – far more powerful than insights and intuitions – that impact upon the purified heart. A Prophet is the ultimate model of conduct for evolving human beings in that he acts in the right way, at the right time and in a manner that is most appropriate for the occasion. His way of life is understood and approved by people of intellect, wisdom and insight. He is the complete human.

Prophethood implies transmission, information and messages regarding Divine Truth and knowledge of the Creator's essence, attributes and creational ways, as well as boundaries necessary for correct behaviour. Several prophets and messengers conveyed instructions regarding boundaries, appropriate conduct and prescribed laws. A prophet's personal conduct and actions always reflected the best of human qualities such as generosity, courage, modesty, justice, gentleness, firmness, wisdom and other commendable virtues. His leadership and care for fellow human beings encompassed the weak, the needy, the good as well as the mischievous. He is especially close to those who are serious in the quest of gnosis. The life of the prophetic being reflects the proper path to the knowledge of God and enlightenment.

All prophets and messengers were endowed with miracles and other inexplicable qualities appropriate to their time and mission. The miracle of the Prophet Muhammad is the Qur'an and his noble way of living amongst the anarchic and brutal Arabian tribes.

The way and life of the Prophet Muhammad, his conduct, practices and teachings are a living illustration of the Qur'an. The outer human difficulties and afflictions of the Prophet are understandable in the light of the revolutionary changes he brought. The Prophet's sacrifices in fulfilling the Divine mission become negligibly insignificant compared to the inner delights and Divine intimacies he received. When the inner battle is won, the outer, physical struggles are only a small price to pay.

The Prophet Mohammed had said that there were thousands of prophets but the Qur'an mentions the following names (in Arabic with the English equivalent):

| | | | |
|---|---|---|---|
| Adam* | Adam | Lut | Lot |
| Al-Yasa | Elisha; | Musa* | Moses |
| Ayyub | Job | Muhammad | |
| Dawud | David | Nuh | Noah |
| Harun | Aaron | Saleh | Salih |
| Hizqil | Ezekiel | Shu'ayb | Jethro |
| Hud | Eber/Heber | Sulayman* | Solomon |
| Ibrahim* | Abraham | Uzair | Ezra |
| Idris | Enoch | Yahya | John |
| Ilyas | Elias | Yaqub | Jacob |
| Isa* | Jesus | Yunus | Jonah |
| Ishaq | Isaac | Yusuf | Joseph |
| Ismail | Ishmael | Zakariyah | Zachariah |

*Traditionally in Islam, these five prophets are referred to as the 'Resolute Messengers'.

The Qur'an declares that the essence of the prophets' messages was the same — that of God's unity and Lordship over all of creation and that the purpose of human life is to submit to God's perfect will and live in preparation for the hereafter. Outer differences between prophets are due to the time and culture of their people.

The Qur'an dwells mostly upon Abraham's lineage and prophets that were relevant to people in the Middle East and the Mediterranean region.

## 6.1 Many Prophets with One Message

The Prophets Noah, Abraham, Moses and numerous others before Jesus have all revealed that the essence and power of life is One God who had created the universe and human beings to submit to this truth and practice transformative worship in preparation for the hereafter. Over thousands of years, these enlightened beings disclosed what was revealed to them about the sacred light and its presence throughout the universe. They spoke the language of their people and addressed worldly issues as relevant to their cultures, highlighting the purpose of man and the privilege of stewardship and its responsibility for all creation.

The duties of man on earth include humility, charitable deeds and constant remembrance of God, His generosity and mercy. Access to God consciousness is through faith, submission and obedience to God's will. Service and help to others with selflessness coupled with supplication, prayers and worship has been a repeated prescription by the prophets. Salvation can only occur by abandonment of love for wealth and power and the realisation of the sacred presence in all that is seen and unseen.

The prophets mentioned in the Qur'an represent a small portion of many others who came to other people and cultures in ancient times. These prophets are considered a brotherhood in enlightenment following in the footsteps of the ancient ones like Noah and Abraham.

## 6.2 Different Cultures and People

Cultures and languages evolved as human beings spread throughout the earth and settled in fertile lands in clusters of clans and communities. Prophets and messengers arose from amongst these different peoples to explain the purpose of life and God's will and governance. Seafaring people were shown aspects of God's presence differently to land-based, agricultural settlements. To expound about God's ways in creation, the specific culture and way of life needs to be used as a backdrop to the religious ideas and teachings and transformation.

There is a clear, unifying thread in the messages of all prophets, with differences in the historical and cultural context of their time. The essence and inner meaning of all of these messages were the same regarding the oneness that is the power and source of energy in the universe. The differences are often to do with the needs of the people and their culture. Greater differences appear due to the passage of time and human interpretation (or misinterpretation) of the prescriptions that were given and their context.

The prophets' main role was to bring concepts such as justice and accountability for all, individually as well as collectively. They all warned against arrogance, pride and oppression of the weak and the poor. Generosity, charity and good conduct are a main feature of these messages. God is the all-generous and gives to all; it is the human duty to reflect some of these Divine attributes on earth.

## 6.3 Prophetic Qualities

The Prophets' character and conduct are considered as the ultimate example for the faithful seekers to emulate. According to their time and culture, each prophet acted most appropriately in their duties. Stewardship on earth or vice-regency was lived at every level by these most evolved beings who connected the lights of the unseen with the seen. Acts of miracles and profound utterances were normal to them. They lived in this world, whilst strongly conscious of the sacred Source that governs the universe in utter perfection: they acted as normal human beings but were plugged into the source of all knowledge and unveilings.

Virtues of generosity, patience, compassion, kindness and gentleness were a common denominator of all of these beings. They also stood firmly when it came to the purpose of this life and the way to God. They lived in truth throughout their lives and were harder upon themselves than upon anyone else. Their inflexible faith, trust and commitment to God surpassed every other consideration. They never asked for worldly rewards, power or wealth and their constant concern was to uplift the less fortunate of creation, with special care for woman, the elderly and children.

Prophets and messengers were the ultimate role models for their people and for mankind on a whole. The Abrahamic prophets have all reinforced each others' messages and the last prophet of that line — Muhammad — reiterated the truth that went before him, while updating the religious prescriptions. Through selfless conduct and awareness of Allah's incomparable justice and perfection, the Muslim seeker is confident in achieving a good destiny.

## 6.4 Courage and Sacrifice of Prophets

True friends of God have no fear, nor do they grieve. Prophets are the first rank friends and servants of God. In paradise, everything is perfect, without any discord. On earth, we are challenged constantly to act as wisely and selflessly as we can, whilst maintaining true commitment or reliance upon God. Prophets and messengers are exposed to a greater share of afflictions and difficulties, because their messages are uncommon, especially their attempts to bring heavenly light upon earthly darkness. People's resistance and their enmity are often forceful and violent.

The worst opposition to the Prophets was from the leaders of their own communities and other wealthy individuals. When a community degenerates, its leaders tend to oppress the weak and the poor and dominate people's lives. It is mostly during such dark times that prophets came to revive the human purpose on earth. Thus, they were denied by their own people and the leaders of the decaying communities were their main enemies.

The Prophet Muhammad was accused of madness and of being a soothsayer; his few early followers were amongst the poorest within the community. After many years of persecution and oppression endured with much sacrifice and courage, they left Mecca for Medina.

The path of God consciousness requires turning away from the lower self. The path of the unseen is the other side of that which is tangible and earthly. The Prophets' mission is to remind human beings of the hereafter and the need to live with faith, conviction, selfless dedication and worship as wayfarers on their journey to the hereafter. They strived without coercion or earthly expectations of rewards. They were the perfect role models for their people and their memory remains alive eternally.

## 6.5 Living Islam

After centuries of war between the greatest powers on earth, the Romans and the Persians, the time was ripe for a fresh reminder to mankind of the path of God consciousness through faithful submission and worship.

The admission of human inadequacy and dependency is the first step towards spiritual growth. This arose through the prophetic light of Muhammad. Islam means to surrender to this realisation, accompanied by complete faith and trust in the One. Good acts and the experience of the generosity and grace of God upon all of creation are preludes to the knowledge that God knows and sees whatever we think or do — all of which will affect our lives. All prophets and messengers carried this message of original Islam.

Islamic worship leads to the realisation of sacred presence of the one God by watchfulness of egotistic vices and purification of the heart. God consciousness will lift the seeker to the highest level of human potential and entry into the domain of stewardship. This was the teaching of all prophets, who upheld outer bounds, laws and justice for all.

Islam proclaims that there is no reality other than the one and only God and that if we sincerely ask we will find answers. The human being is the microcosm that can reflect every aspect of the macrocosm. Thus, he is at the peak of creation with the greatest responsibility and potential for consciousness and knowledge.

The path of Islam is that of constant remembrance of the one original Light. Islam prescribes one to live cautiously, with modesty and great hope in this transitory life, awaiting the eternal state of the hereafter.

## 6.6 Equity, Charity and Justice

God's justice is to give all of Adam's offspring an equal opportunity to reach their highest spiritual potential. The weak and meek especially should be helped and assisted for the sake of all.

It is human nature to have needs and desires throughout life. Biological evolution is a precursor to spiritual evolvement and knowledge of Allah's sacred presence. Whoever is in tune with God consciousness will naturally be concerned about helping others who have not attained that higher state in life. Justice implies having a social and political situation that enables every human being to reach as high as possible along the journey of God consciousness. The Prophet had shown much concern for the poor and needy, especially orphans, women and the elderly.

The poor tax in religion is designated for those who are unable to earn their keep. To do one's utmost in charitable action is an important aspect of living Islam and a big factor in control of egotism and love of wealth and luxury.

All prophets and messengers emphasised the need for attention to the weaker members of society. For those who are enlightened, there is no 'otherness' in truth and the needy person one meets is reflecting the inner impoverishment within us. To help the needy is to help one's own self along its journey of discovery of one's soul — the sacred essence of God.

## 6.7 Laws and Boundaries

God has created everything according to a measure, each with its own limitations. If we transgress the natural limits or boundaries, then we are risking injury, even irrevocable damage.

The outer natural drive for freedom from limitations implies the existence of boundaries and outer limitations. Inner freedom and joy can only be contained within clearly defined borders. For that reason, both at the individual as well as the societal levels, we need to adhere to a recognised system of law and order. Balance, equilibrium and peace are desirable at all levels.

A serious Muslim will realise the wisdom of boundaries of what is permissible and what is not, both ritualistically as well as according to customs and habits of the Prophet Muhammad and his faithful followers.

Certain matters are clearly good and others are not; the areas of doubt and uncertainty in between are best avoided until clarification is sought. Scholarship and relevant reference to the Islamic laws and jurisprudence are essential.

Whatever is discerned in the universe exists within some limitations imposed by time and space. Only God's light and will, however, is free of all limitations. Boundlessness can only be realised within the purified heart, where the soul resides.

It is the intelligent person who accepts whatever governs the society's wellbeing and stability, and then dives into the spiritual boundlessness and the unseen realms. Without acknowledging terrestrial realities and wisdom, celestial lights and insights cannot reliably take place. Adam's descent is only to bring about well-earned ascent.

## 6.8 Religious Rituals and Practices

God declares His closeness and that He will answer those with faith and sincerity in a generous and wise way.

Islam is the path of unity of one's intentions, actions and higher expectations. It begins with a declaration by tongue, reflecting a sincere heart. A Muslim is he who confesses that there is one God and that Muhammad is the Messenger. Our natural needs in life will make us supplicate, invocate and pray for God's power to relieve us from needs, pains and fears. Communal supplications and prayers increase the possibility of good outcomes.

There are special occasions, times and seasons that are auspicious: such as the nights of power during the month of fasting, Ramadan. There are also sacred places where acts of worship are enhanced. The symbolic house of God was established by the Prophet Abraham in Mecca, where people circumambulated and prayed in its vicinity. Jerusalem was also a major centre for prayers and pilgrimage. The practices of regular and formal prayers, fasting, payment of poor dues, pilgrimage, performing good actions and exerting outer and inner struggle to reform the self are part of the essential package of Islam.

Cleanliness of body, mind and heart are essential preconditions to acts of prayer and worship. It is important to eat and drink modestly of that which is prescribed as pure and clean. There are clear boundaries and restrictions on our senses and actions.

It is important for human beings to realise that we need God's grace and mercy at all times, and that it can be received when we are ready and receptive. Restrictions and shortages are part of God's ways to limit our egotistic drive.

It is good for individuals as well as communities to supplicate, pray, fast and perform other acts of worship as frequently as possible. To be closer to God (whose Light covers the whole universe) it is necessary to turn away from the confusion in our minds and surroundings. God consciousness and deep reflection are the goals of the sincere seeker.

## 6.9 Relationships, Duties and Courtesies

God orders us to be gentle and courteous to our parents and elders. Acknowledgement and respect for our biological roots are a step towards realising our spiritual origin.

Islam reveals the appropriate paths for correct relationships and duties towards people and God. We have duties towards parents, neighbours, humanity and all of creation. There has to be clear boundaries in personal relationships in gender. A family must be respected and strengthened. Ultimately, relationships between human beings will reach their best level when people realise that every heart contains a sacred soul that is the same as every other human soul. If the individual has not submitted to the inner ruler — the soul — then to exercise authority over others will only bring about greater disorder. Whoever is not under control is not fit to bring order to others. A good action multiplies tenfold, whereas wrong action will only bring about its equivalent reaction.

Marriage between man and woman is an attempt to unify complimentary opposites, therefore there is an element of sacredness in the act. If, however, due to earthly reasons the relationship is not workable, then an amicable separation is acceptable. To exercise courtesies towards others and to be kind and helpful is in fact a generosity towards one's own real self. Self-concern can only increase the egotistic tendencies whilst with concern for others' wellbeing, one is on the path towards understanding similarities that lead to unity in essence.

It is important, as a courtesy to oneself, to be watchful with every thought, intention and action and not to waste time or energy in speculation of frivolous actions and risky gambles. The ultimate courtesy is to live fully in the moment and to have insights to the perfections therein. Contentment here and now reflects an aspect of the perfection of the Creator of all space and time. If one's relationship with God is right, then all other relationships will fit in appropriately.

## 6.10 Perfect Worship

Our earthly life is the training ground for the ascent in consciousness back to perfect unity. Unless we have done our preparatory work in this life, we will be much handicapped in the realms of the hereafter. If we do not develop spiritual insights and wisdom in this world, we will be like the blind and the dumb in the next.

At the original point of creation, everything was in total unity before any apparent diversity. At the end of creation, all returns to that unity. It is from the source of original gatheredness, before dispersion, that the fields and streams of love overflow. The whole universe is held by forces of affinity and relationships based on the essence of primal love. All human passions or obsessions are earthly manifestations of the original sacred love.

Worship implies boundless adoration and willingness to sacrifice everything for the sake of what is worshipped. It is also an expression of personal need and inadequacy, and a declaration of hope to reach ultimate contentment and happiness through that love.

Acts of worship benefit people in ways and according to the

extent of their knowledge of the Lord they worship. In truth, we are all equal in front of God, but will be judged according to the extent of our God consciousness. At the worldly level, acts of worship can soften the heart and reduce egotistic drives.

Proper worship will highlight the importance of acting appropriately and accountably in the outer world whilst emphasising preparation for the hereafter. Through transformative worship we realise that human destiny can only be fulfilled by the realisation of Perfect Divine governance, presence and prevalence throughout the universe.

It is perfect worship that produces perfect God consciousness. The Prophet Muhammad emphasised that an hour of deep reflection or meditation is better than seventy years of formal worship.

## 6.11 The Way of Muhammad

Muhammad was sent as a witness of Truth, giver of good news (of the One merciful God) and warnings, to call people to Allah and as a beacon of light to show the path to salvation.

At his mature age of 40, and during a night of fasting, the Qur'an was revealed to the heart of the Prophet as a mercy for all of mankind. He was concerned for all people and compassionate to the believers, whilst firm with those who rejected that the purpose of life is to know and worship the one God. He was an orphan and not formally tutored, but had a strong, intuitive sense with the spoken and written word. He was not interested in wealth or power and had no personal egotistic motives. He was just and kind to all, including his enemies. He had rejected all the inhumane habits and traditions of his people, but maintained and reformed those customs that were appropriate for human evolvement. He had acknowledged all the Prophets before him, but rejected the deviations and distortions in their teachings that had taken place due to human tendencies for corruption.

After years of difficulties and persecution in Mecca, he was invited by the people of Medina to emigrate there, where a small community began to grow. During this period, laws and regulations were produced for the stability of this new society. There was much tribal mischief in the early years in Medina concerning the loyalty of people and the breakdown of treaties and agreements. Formal prayers and other acts of worship were established in Medina and the direction of prayers was changed from Jerusalem to Mecca. The inner strength of this small community brought about unparalleled outer power and courage, through unity of purpose and direction. The Qur'an was fully revealed and the pilgrimage to Mecca sealed the Prophetic message. Muhammad's conduct was the Qur'an in practice, thus he was the ultimate example of a being who perfected the meaning of Adam's descent to earth and ascent back to the Garden.

## 6.12 Humanity and Divinity

Allah promises His special grace and favour upon His messengers and their people. The angels too confirm their obedience to the Lord.

All Prophets and Messengers lived and taught amongst their own people and what distinguishes them was a subtle but powerful quality of connectedness to the Supreme consciousness of God. They were earthly beings guided by heavenly insights. They warned against distraction and loss and gave the good news that whoever lives faithfully with trust, and acts in a manner that is guided by God consciousness, has redeemed themselves. The Prophet Jesus exemplified the human paradox of how humanity and divinity connect in one being. He was human, but fully absorbed in God Consciousness. Intrinsically, all human beings aspire to that state — to be in this world, but to know they are not confined to it.

The heart contains the sacred and mysterious soul that is the source of our life, caused by the spirit of God that holds the Universe along its journey. It is through the soul that human beings have consciousness of lights, shadows and all other discernible entities. Children of Adam are warned as to how Satan caused their parents to be expelled out of paradise. We are also shown that it is only through faithfulness and selfless acts with a humble heart that we can reclaim the lost state of the garden. Prophets and eternal beings were transformed through God Consciousness and awareness of the eternal Oneness that is the essence of all creation. Thus, their hearts were joyful and their deeds were for the good of all.

Divinity is thinly veiled by the universe and its diversity and by the outer human identity and apparent separation. In truth, it is divinity that brings life and potential awakening to human beings. We are heavenly in soul and earthly in body.

## 6.13 Universal Mercy and Grace

Grace and mercy cascade from Allah, bringing life and consciousness to all of creation. All Messengers and Prophets are manifestations of God's generosity and Lordship — a mercy to human beings.

God is the source of whatever appears and whatever is unseen. He is the Ultimate Guide, the All-knower and the Bestower of all the goodness that we ask for. Those who trust, have faith in these sacred attributes and act with good intentions will experience God's guidance, mercy and compassion. Grace can only be experienced by those who act cautiously, access God consciousness and perform all their duties. These are the keys to the ever-present Mercy.

Fear and hope are the two most important motivators for human life on earth. We naturally desire wellbeing at numerous personal levels, as well as that of society. The more one is in cautious awareness of the egotistic pitfalls and dangers, the more one experiences hope and clarity in direction. Happiness is the outcome of least desires or expectations from creation combined with constant reliance and witnessing of the ever-present Divine grace and perfections.

The Prophet Noah warned his people that due to their wrong actions, they would be overtaken by a natural disaster that would wipe out all the transgressors. He accepted the disaster as a necessary, just outcome. We all try to exercise and experience goodness on earth and avoid evil.

God is the source of perfect and absolute goodness and justice. It is up to us to leave our illusions and confusions and witness Allah's mercy and grace in all events and situations by making our defective judgment disappear when the light of His judgment appears.

## Chapter 7

## Salvation and Enlightenment

Introduction
7.1  Information and Transformation
7.2  Special Warnings
7.3  Inner Integrity
7.4  Living Faith
7.5  Path of Relief and Gladness
7.6  Path of Despair and Sadness
7.7  Anchored Transcendence
7.8  Happy Sobriety
7.9  Beyond Ease and Difficulty
7.10  God Consciousness
7.11  Unitive Resonance

# 7

# Salvation and Enlightenment

**Introduction**

Islam is a *'din'* — a word that means debt and obligation, and that implies a debt upon oneself to save yourself from the veils of falsehood, uncertainty, doubt, ignorance and worldly limitations. The path of submission (Islam) begins by realising human shortcomings, inadequacies and desire for happiness. It leads to faith, the need for knowledge, appropriate conduct and action for contentment and wellbeing. The seeker will realise that all basic human desires and motivations lead to a guiding light that is constantly and reliably available and ever-present. Initial submission and faith becomes illumined and transformative.

The conduct of the enlightened Muslim is based upon spontaneous self-awareness and accountability, resulting in a just and healthy community. All of the Islamic practices and laws lead towards heightened awareness, good intentions and appropriate actions. If the Qur'an and way of the Prophets are followed, both in outer form and inner meaning, then without doubt, transformation and awakening occur to higher consciousness. A better quality life will thus take place.

The purpose of all spiritual practices is to leave the domain of earthly roots, be illumined and realise the Divine Presence in every situation and at all times. The Qur'an defines all religions as being based on faithful submission and commitment to the truth. Therefore, the original message of every prophetically inspired religion was an Islamic message, though each was given a different name, at a different time, for a different people. All Prophets and Messengers professed the same truth and reflected the needs of their people appropriately. The message was one of good news — God alone rules the universe, but unless this perfect leadership is realised, the bad news is suffering and hardship will prevail.

The fountain of Islam is transformative worship and appropriate conduct towards oneself (the lower and the higher self), creation and the Creator. The final message of Islam as relayed by the Prophet Muhammad contains all that is needed for spiritual health and enlightenment for all peoples at all times.

The teachings, practices and rituals of Islam contain great disciplines for breaking normative behaviour and unhealthy habits. The limitations and restrictions that these practices and rituals impose upon personal conduct are extremely beneficial as they facilitate spiritual development and higher consciousness. As an example, the outer difficulties of fasting provide a great deal of awareness and sensitivity that illumine the heart and open it to wisdom, guidance, compassion, patience and tolerance; outer difficulties, hardships and change of habits can lead the faithful seeker towards rewarding progress along the path of enlightenment.

God's perfection overflows throughout the universe and manifests on earth as nature's wonders, ecological interlinks and harmonies. The human stewardship and responsibility implies attention, respect, and concern for all creation. By conscious watchfulness, we can grow beyond egotistic veils of misconception and shallow understanding. If we desire a life of grace, with the least amount of personal and social affliction, we must act according to Divine intention and design. The sincere seeker is in a state of constant self-awareness, accountability, humility and realisation of the nearness of death.

Allah has revealed that He is a hidden treasure and "He loved to be known — thus He Created". This sacred treasury can only be realised if one embraces higher attributes and qualities and sublimates the lower human tendencies. The lower self and its tendencies bestow some humility upon us so that we may take refuge in God's mercy, forgiveness and generosity.

The sincere seeker is honest, forthright and pursues his urgent need for spiritual growth and awakening. He reads the Qur'an and reflects upon Allah's commands and prohibitions, as directed primarily to himself. To live the Qur'an is to move higher in true life.

Stability for the human being means inner contentment and sustainable happiness. The driving forces in life are the power of attraction towards what is liked and repulsion away from what is disliked. If the self is not educated and groomed in wisdom and pursuit of the higher self and enlightenment, then it will naturally slide towards the lower self and its conditioned consciousness.

Allah's love for Adam and his offspring implies that natural patterns and designs in creation are all conducive for growth towards the knowledge of the Lord through self-knowledge. From there on, the awakened heart can take beautiful flights and discoveries in the realm of lights, insights and spiritual thrills.

## 7.1 Information and Transformation

Our senses, mind, intellect and heart links our lower self to our higher self. Our senses connect us to the outer world and are coordinated through the inner sense that feeds into the faculty of imagination, reflection and thinking — the mind. We are naturally inquisitive and curious, and desire to acquire more knowledge and information, much of which is useful for day-to-day existence and survival. On subtler levels, information may bring about a connection between the ego and the higher self and trigger transformation in consciousness. All information or knowledge is an opportunity for a shift in consciousness.

Generally, information gives us some idea or knowledge about an outer situation. We often know through self-awareness when we act arrogantly or selfishly, and it is only when knowledge is internalised and has become a part of one's mental reference, that transformation occurs.

For the faithful believer in God's mercy and generosity, information is referred to God consciousness and is either discarded or energised by the inner lights of the soul. Transformed beings see with eyes and insights, and hear with ears, as well as their hearts. This state becomes like a torchlight in one's hand along the dark and treacherous earthly pathways. We use our mind and senses during our journey in life and respond to insights and openings which are beyond definitions or reason. We respond to outer information and messages which eventually lead us to the zone of the heart and the lights of the soul – transformation to another state.

## 7.2 Special Warnings

A wise person is ever-watchful of the lower self and is never secure in what he knows. An enlightened person is secure in God's generosity and the Divine grace that gives him what he needs to know at the right time — Allah is the true Guide. The human duty is to be vigilant in misguidance and distractions and to ensure a wholesome and gentle heart.

Errors and mistakes are inevitable; they are part of one's growth and learning in this life. The danger is that there are certain mistakes that leave their negative mark indefinitely upon us. We are warned that troubles and afflictions far away may reach people, who are at a distance from the perpetrators. We are also warned to recognise that simple faith and belief in God, though necessary conditions, are insufficient to bring about a conducively just and healthy environment for a community. We need to shun all transgressions, aggressions, violence, immodesty, wasteful living, disloyalty, arrogance and other vices.

Every individual weaves his own cocoon of desires and attachments that will detract from spiritual growth. The lower self will always bring about excuses for delays and procrastinations to avoid yielding to the light within the heart. We love immortality but we translate that into leaving behind earthly markers or monuments and forget the truth that the soul within the heart is itself immortal. We always follow the path of comfort and ease, rather than put up with restrictions and boundaries, which may bring about faster spiritual growth.

Trouble and turmoil on earth are entirely due to human mischief and distraction from the path of God consciousness and readiness for the hereafter. Allah will draw the wrongdoers in ways that we do not comprehend, sometimes through greater worldly wealth, entrapment and fancy illusions. Even religion has been used for worldly purposes individually and collectively. The human tendency is to reduce pure consciousness to conditioned human levels.

## 7.3 Inner Integrity

Allah is One, Unique and Incomparable. Human knowledge of Allah's unity is through unison between the mind and heart, or the ego and soul. When that happens, the person becomes wholesome and integrated, and will truly understand God's Oneness. We care for the proper growth and development of a child and hope for wholesomeness in character. Outer growth and behaviour are necessary in human evolvement, but ultimately, it is the condition of the heart, its faith, its purity and trust, and reliance on God's presence and guidance that will lead to spiritual awakening. Outer skills and wisdom are necessary preludes to awareness of the inner light and God consciousness — inner wisdom.

A developed mind and intellect can also be tricky and deceitful. It takes conscious will and determination to be always truthful and transparent. Animals use camouflage and deception as part of their survival instinct and natural evolutionary growth. For humans, who have been exposed to the sacred light of the Creator and therefore seek higher consciousness, there is no excuse for hypocrisy and deception.

It is natural for us to be unhappy if we have accumulated many attachments, anger, fears and hatred in our hearts. A healthy person would like to be clear-minded and pure at heart. We don't like to carry regrets that we cannot overcome or put right. The path of unity implies love, compassion, loyalty and other appropriate conduct in order that the lower self yields to the higher. Then we become integrated and feel a sense of personal unity. If an individual has not attained inner Oneness within him/herself, then doubt will remain with ensuing confusion in intentions and actions. The spiritual paths help to bring about inner harmony, balance and contentment and thereby, human integrity and Oneness that results in blissfulness in Allah's Oneness.

## 7.4 Living Faith

To absorb the message of the Qur'an fully and be transformed by it, is like coming out of darkness into light — a new state of consciousness. From childhood, we experience different levels of faith and trust, as we rely upon parents and other people. The sparks of generosity, selfless service and love all begin with the mother's response to the baby's needs. The injured child cries for help in the hope and trust that help will soon come.

A mature person relies on his own abilities as well as upon others. In addition, the religious person relies upon God's unseen powers and mercy. The spiritually wise person is always patient and trusts that the ultimate outcome of every situation is a destiny that needs to be read and accepted.

Faith and trust works at the causal worldly level as well as that which we do not know about — the unseen. That is why this world is an intermediate stage that trains us with what is discernible, so that we can face and be at peace with what is intangible. It is through living faith that we can straddle both humanity and divinity in perfect balance. Every human being is given opportunities to admit failure and ignorance so that faith and trust in God is increased and deepened. This profound transformative experience cannot be just passed from one person to another but has to be lived and internalised. Faith has to be lived in all facets of life for it to be transformative.

The love for Prophets or enlightened people can open up the channels for the wide spectrum of faith and knowledge that there is one perfect Governor of everything in the universe — Allah the Lord of All. The Prophet Abraham asked God to show him how the living comes out of the dead so that his heart would become rooted in that faith. Muslims are along that same path.

## 7.5 Path of Relief and Gladness

Lasting relief and security can only be attained through transformative faith and God consciousness. Mature human beings can be absorbed in their worldly life without concern regarding death and what comes thereafter. People of religious faith and belief will look for signs along their path that may increase their trust, faith and knowledge of God. As for those who are diligently watchful of the pitfalls of the lower self and have committed themselves to acts of goodness, they certainly will get their signs of encouragement in this life. Then, there are those who live their faith and always act as well as they can because their heart is humble and illumined by God consciousness. They certainly experience joy and bliss in this world as preludes to the eternal garden after death. For the enlightened being, there are two levels of gardens — worldly and heavenly.

Early on in one's life, the burdensome lower self asserts itself until maturity and old age, when wisdom and greater insights show the way out from that *cul-de-sac*. Early submission and a concept of faith could lead, ultimately, to the realisation of the Divine presence and total relief from all worldly illusions and delusions. Generally, the spiritual path begins with difficulty, but with persistence there is no doubt that the seeker will live an illumined and joyful life, content in the knowledge that Allah is the perfect guide throughout this earthly passage.

For people on this path, faith, courage and love of truth are the weapons of the seeker. The true religious path is the way of deliverance from a journey that is fraught with dangerous distractions and pitfalls leading to the joyful vistas of the soul.

## 7.6 Path of Despair and Sadness

Without faith, trust or a reliable path to lead us out of the natural worldly confusions, despair will be the obvious outcome. If we don't reflect upon and understand the patterns and laws that govern life, we will undoubtedly face a bleak outcome. To simply pursue short-lived pleasures in this world is easy to begin with, but will bring about a regrettable end. A child who postpones immediate pleasures is considered more intelligent than the one who grabs whatever is on offer. The ultimate wisdom is patience and unity with the state of the hereafter.

People who are totally engrossed in the world will only remember and be concerned about the world's materialistic pursuits. They do not reflect upon higher meanings and meditate beyond the mental box, so are confined to the limited and conditioned consciousness. These people do not see the Creator's signs and the amazing interplay in creation that is moving along a direction towards the Source from which it emanated — the glorious Lord of all.

A person who lives without faith or without trust in the One generally does not enjoy the experience and witnessing of the wide horizon of mercy and grace that envelops the universe. Hardened hearts, self-centred desires and love for wealth and power eventually block spiritual growth and insight. In societies that have gone astray, the excuse is often given that this was the way and the culture of their forefathers.

Traditional habits and the continuity of customs give the lower self a sense of constancy. This is how we can justify some of our foolish acts as good. The path of despair may be attractive as far as its outer appearance is concerned, but is, without doubt, fringed with sadness, fear and uncertainty. Without a living transformative faith, the grim end can only be symbolised as eternal fire.

## 7.7 Anchored Transcendence

The self longs for freedom from spatial and temporal limitations. The soul belongs to the realm of boundless joy and bliss. The self must transcend to the soul, if it is to be fully content and happy.

Human nature evolves with physical, mental and intellectual growth and then begins to aspire to the gifts of the heart and the soul therein. As part of youth and maturity, we want to interact and succeed in the outer world with reason and understanding. Worldly experiences and wisdom are a good rock bed upon which to build higher wisdom and insights. We find at the base of the human make-up the four substances of earth, water, fire and air. We have solid bones with channels of blood that flow within us, heating and cooling mechanisms transfer energy from the outside to our bodies, then our total dependence on air is measured in minutes. Our earthly anchor needs to be fairly secure and in equilibrium before we can progress along higher realms of consciousness. To be healthy in body, mind and heart is essential for spiritual wellbeing.

Earthly existence is totally dependent upon light and heat that is constantly being regenerated from the sun and other chemical reactions. Accompanying the original Light is consciousness with its vast spectrum. It is only the human being that can have simple awareness and mental remembrances, as well as God consciousness and transcendence, beyond all discernable limitations. To know this world well is to sample some of its gross aspects, which may lead to the subtler realms and higher meanings.

The children of Adam are all perched temporarily on earth, whilst constantly seeking the state of their origin beyond death — the garden of paradise. The wholesome life is that which acknowledges the earthly foundations, but can access the zone of pure consciousness and Divine presence. In truth, there is no separation between these two oceans that meet at the heart of the seeker.

## 7.8 Happy Sobriety

Intoxication implies a transition from a normal state of awareness to another state, where reason and rationality are not operative. This state of consciousness occurs naturally at the point of death or is induced by intoxicants. Happiness, however, is due to contentment and certainty of God's perfect guidance and generosity.

Human drives for freedom from earthly limitations and love for overcoming boundaries indicate a tendency within us to seek states of consciousness that are not normal or common on earth. The prohibition of alcohol for the seeker is clearly due to its negative side-effects.

There is no doubt, however, that intoxication can easily change human consciousness into another zone, beyond the normal. We quest greater knowledge and higher consciousness, understandings and insights. We also seek meaning from dreams and other subconscious influences and look for explanations of other psychic forces.

Sobriety is rooted in rational, logical mental capacity and is important as a starting point towards transcendental experiences. Physical health is often measured by the speed with which we can raise the heart rate as well as drop it. Spiritual health can also be measured according to the ease of transcendence from normal consciousness and return back to it.

Most durable Sufi paths are based on practising sobriety through acceptance and adherence to outer laws and regulations, then entering into a state of God consciousness and higher awareness. We are connected to the physical world through hearing, sight and other senses, and the unseen world through insights and intuitions of the soul. These two states are closely connected for the enlightened person. The faithful Muslim is promised temporary blissful states on earth before permanent paradise in the next life.

## 7.9 Beyond Ease and Difficulty

Ease and difficulty, like good and bad, are natural experiences that are unavoidable on earth. We try to reduce what is undesirable and attract what we consider to be good. Human intentions and actions are energised by this interplay of opposites — vices and virtues.

We can never exclude difficulties in our lives, nor should we stop in our attempts to eradicate them. The answer lies in acceptance of the nature of worldly patterns of experience, and transcendence to higher consciousness.

The gardens we create on earth are like trial runs for the state of the garden in heaven. It is through reflection, meditation, prayer and patience that we can access the state of inner bliss and happiness at heart — beyond all ease or difficulty.

The lower self loves ease and comfort, whilst the soul urges transformation. Life is the urgent pursuit of its source — the life-giving soul. People of faith and trust in God and in the hereafter are always aware of the possibility that their life may end before attaining the truth. The wise seeker is always self-critical, is hard upon his or her own self, is lenient with others and is always asking forgiveness from the Creator for lack of appropriate intentions and actions.

With constant remembrance of God and reliance upon His grace in all situations, awareness and reference are exercised where the unison between the self and soul will take one beyond ease and comfort, to the joy of witnessing the perfection of Divine will. That state of spiritual maturity combines both earthly and heavenly wisdom and the delights of praising the glorious qualities of the Lord of the universe.

## 7.10 God Consciousness

There is no God but God and Muhammad is the messenger of God to remind humankind that the purpose of life on earth is to realise this transformative truth. For nearly a third of our life, the child in us grows and develops its personality and ego. The second third is the interactive phase with other people to realise differences and similarities.

In essence, everyone desires a similar outcome — sustained happiness, but along different paths. The third stage relates to wisdom and God consciousness and the transcendental realities. We start life by learning about the outer world through our senses and the mind, and with maturity, we need to know about subtler worlds and the inner soul.

God consciousness is the ultimate stage in the evolution of

mankind and is beyond causality and limitations. If we relate life to consciousness, then it has many levels and degrees: the ant is alive, so are the fox, the baboon and human beings. Each of these animals is at a different level of awareness. Only human beings can connect with the highest levels of consciousness.

The Qur'an says that by faithful commitment to this truth you will come to live a true life that can only be attained through God consciousness and the realisation of the immense majesty and beauty of the Creator.

The path to this awakening is through proper religious conduct, dedicated actions and liberation from the lower self. Spiritual righteousness cannot be attained until all love and attachments for anything other than Allah have vanished. God consciousness is the gateway to the realm of paradise — here, now and forever.

## 7.11 Unitive Resonance

The Universe and all of creation praises Allah — the incomparable One. The Divine qualities, names or attributes are like a field of energy that permeate creation and gives every entity a sense of direction. Human beings love and adore God through all of His glorious qualities and attributes, which are countless and relate to each other at the highest level. At this point of Oneness, it is love that fuses them all and that is how we experience how diverse entities or opposites meet in unity. He is the one Real that is self-sustaining and envelops the whole universe, which is encompassed within the limitations of space and time.

Adam descended from the realm of perfect boundlessness in order to rise again and return back to that state of eternal paradise. From that One cosmic source multitudes of qualities and attributes emerged that are like fields of energy that envelop conscious creations.

God's sacred, unifying light permeates all that is known and unknown and appears at numerous levels of diffusions and fusions. The human soul has had exposure to and knowledge of the original Light and is, therefore, sacred. To kill one person unjustly is like murdering all people and to bring life to one person is like giving life to all humanity.

All human souls are created with the same potential. Once the lower self is harnessed, then the person is far from the confusion of 'otherness' and is secure in 'Oneness'.

God's supreme consciousness and light overflows into multitudes of channels that manifest as energies, matter and physical entities — all of which carry the memory of the original state of unity, and yearn for it.

The ultimate spiritual experience is to resonate with Allah's supreme light through God consciousness — the station to which we all aspire.

# Qur'anic References

The Qur'an conveys all aspects of the absolute reality and truth and the connections in creation to the eternal essence. There are numerous levels and colours in the tapestry of the Qur'an and many issues are shown from different angles and perspectives. The topics covered in this book have numerous references in different contextual frameworks. The following references have been selected as an illustration of the source from which the main text was derived. A Qur'anic scholar may find other verses that can also shed light on the issues under discussion. Therefore, the referenced verses are not exhaustive.

On average, every sub-chapter in the book consists of ten to twelve verses with direct reference to it. The translation of these verses is a contemporary version of the publicly available translations and renderings. The emphasis in these translations was the ease of understanding for a reader who is not familiar with the language and the culture of the Qur'an.

# Chapter 1
# Qur'an and Revelation

## 1.1 The Book of Signs and Metaphors

And it is He who has created the heavens and the earth in accordance, with truth and on the day of resurrection, He will say "Be" and it is... He is the knower of the seen and the unseen, All Wise, All Aware. [6:73]

...Clear evidence has come to you from your Lord, this she-camel from Allah is a sign for you, so leave her alone to graze on God's earth and do not harm her, or painful punishment will afflict you. [7:73]

...And Allah sets forth metaphors for mankind so that they may reflect. [14:25]

And consider how your Lord revealed to the bee: build for yourself dwellings in mountains and trees... [16:68]

And We have established the night and the day as two signs... [17:12]

And indeed We have given in this Qur'an every kind of similitude... [17:89]

The metaphor of those who take other than God as protectors is like the spider which makes a house for itself, the flimsiest of all houses is the spider's house... [29:41]

And so We propound these metaphors to man, but none grasp their inner meaning except those who are aware (of truth). [29:43]

## 1.2 The Book of Guidance and Truth

This is the book in which there is no doubt; in it is guidance for all God conscious people. [2:2]

All Mankind were once a single community, then Allah sent prophets with good news and as warners and through them revelation with truth to decide between people regarding their differences... God guides to a straight way whom He wills. [2:213]

And hold fast all of you together, to the rope of Allah and do not be divided...He brought your hearts together, so that through His blessing you become brothers...So that you might find guidance. [3:103]

Who feared the Most Gracious in the unseen and has come with a heart full of repentance. [50:33]

And if it distresses you that those who do not believe turn their backs... (Remember) that it is God who willed it... Therefore do not be like the ignorant ones.) [6:35]

When Allah decides to guide someone, He expands his breast to submission and whoever He wills to veer astray... Like this does God inflict horror upon those who do not believe. [6:125]

It is He who has sent His Apostle with the (task of spreading) guidance and the religion of truth... [9:33]

Say "O Mankind! The truth has now come to you from your Lord. Whoever, chooses to follow the right path, follows it for his own good; and whoever chooses to go astray, he does so to his own loss. And I am not responsible for your conduct". [10:108]

And on the day (of resurrection) We shall raise up from every community a witness against them...This Book is revealed to you providing guidance and mercy and good news to all who have surrendered themselves to God. [16:89]

Verily, this Qur'an guides to all that is just and right and gives the believers who do good actions the good news that theirs will be a great reward. [17:9]

Whoever chooses to follow the right path follows it for his own good and whoever goes astray goes astray to his own loss and no bearer of burdens shall be made to bear another's burden. Moreover, We would not punish (any community) until we have sent an apostle (to them). [17:15]

A guidance (to the right path) and a good news to the believers. [27:2]

Nothing occurs on earth, or in your selves, unless it is (laid down) in Our decree before We bring it into being: certainly, all this is easy for God. [57:22]

## 1.3 The Book of Discrimination and Wisdom

And (remember) when We gave Moses the book and discrimination - so that you may be rightly guided. [2:53]

Our Lord raise up among them a messenger from them, who shall convey your messages and teach them the book and wisdom... You alone are All-Wise. [2:129]

There is no creature that walks the earth and no bird that flies on its two wings which is not in communities like yourselves. We have neglected nothing in the book (decree). Then to their Lord will they be gathered. [6:38]

As for those who deny Our revelations and are arrogant regarding them the gates of heaven will not be open to them and they will not enter the garden until the camel goes through the eye of a needle, this is how We reward the transgressors... [7:40]

We have only revealed the book to you so that you may make clear to them about that which they differ, and a guidance and mercy for people who believe. [16:64]

We have sent down the book to you making all things clear and as a guidance, mercy and good news for the believers. [16:89]

We gave Moses the revelation and made it guidance for the tribe of Israel... [17:2]

And We have sent down this Qur'an (as a source) for wellbeing and as a mercy to those who believe... [17:82]

Blessed is He who revealed to his servant the standard by which to discern the true from the false, so that he may give warning to the entire world. [25:1]

It is Allah who has revealed the book with truth, and a just balance... [42:17]

And the heavens has He raised high, and has devised a measure, so that you may not transgress the measure (of what is right) weigh therefore (your deed) with equity, and do not shortchange on this measure. [55:7-9]

## 1.4  A Universal Book

Your Lord has made mercy incumbent upon himself - so that any who transgress out of ignorance, and then repents and lives righteously, then surely He is All-Forgiving, Merciful. [6:54]

In His possession are the keys to the unseen; no one knows them except Him. He knows all that is on land and sea; not a leaf falls unless He knows it; there is not a grain in the earth's darkness, nor anything moist or dry, which is not recorded in a clear book. [6:59]

Alif Lam Ra. These letters are signs of the Qur'an full of wisdom. [10:1]

This is a book We have revealed to you in order that you might bring mankind out of darkness into the light by permission of their Lord; to the way that leads to the Almighty, the Praiseworthy. [14:1]

We have sent down for you a book, containing all that you ought to bear in mind; will you not, then, use your reason? [21:10]

We have sent you only as (evidence) of mercy towards all the worlds. [21:107]

Those who bear the seat of power of Allah and all who are around it glorify their Lord with praise and believe in Him, and ask forgiveness for all who believe... [40:7]

Certainly this is a reminder for you and your people; and in time you all will be called to account. [43:44]

## 1.5 The Descent of the Qur'an

Any verse, which We abrogate or cause it to be forgotten, We replace it with a better or a similar one. Don't you know that Allah has power over everything. [2:106]

But as for those from among them who are well rooted in knowledge, and the believers who believe in that which has been sent down to you...Who believe in ....

Allah and the last day – We will reward such people immensely. [4:162]

Allah will remove the rage in their hearts. Allah turns to anyone He wills; for God is All-knowing, Wise. [9:15]

Surely it is We who have sent down the "Reminder" and, it is We who will preserve it. [15:9]

And it is a Qur'an which We have gradually unfolded, so that you might read it out to mankind in stages, We revealed it in stages. [17:106]

We did not reveal the Qur'an to you to cause you distress. [20:2]

The faithful spirit has descended with it. [26:193]

Read in the name of your Lord, who created, Created man from a germ-cell! ...

Read - for your Lord is Most Bountiful; who has taught by the pen; taught man what he did not know! [96:1-5]

Surely We have revealed it on the night of Decree; and what will convey what the night of Decree is? The night of Decree is better than a thousand months; Therein descend the angels... [97:1-4]

## 1.6 Approach to the Qur'an

Will they not, then, try to understand this Qur'an? Had it issued from any but God, they would surely have found in it many inner contradictions! [4:82]

And when they listen to the revelation received by the Messenger, you will see their eyes overflowing with tears, for they recognise the truth. They pray "Our Sustainer, we believe, write us down among the witnesses". [5:83]

And when the Qur'an is recited, then listen to it and remain silent, that mercy may be shown to you. [7:204]

Surely (as to) those who believe and do good and humble themselves to their Lord, these are the dwellers of the garden, in it they will abide. [11:23]

Those who listen to the Word and follow the best in it,
Those are the ones whom Allah has guided and those are the ones endowed with understanding. [39:18]

'Do they not then earnestly seek to understand the Qur'an or are their hearts locked up by them?' [47:24]

## 1.7 Other Prophetic Messages

We have made some of these apostles to excel over others, among them are they to whom Allah spoke, and some of them He exalted by (many degrees of) rank; ...And if Allah had pleased, those after them would not have fought one with another after clear arguments had come to them, but they disagreed… [2:253]

But if they reject you, so indeed were rejected before you apostles who came with clear arguments and scriptures and the illuminating book. [3:184]

And We did not send any apostle but that he should be obeyed by Allah's permission… [4:64]

And We have not sent before you but men from (among) the people of the towns, to whom We sent revelations… [12:109]

And We did not send any apostle but with the language of his people, so that he might explain to them clearly… [14:4]

And certainly We raised in every nation an apostle saying: Serve Allah and shun transgression. So there were some of them whom Allah guided and there were others against whom error was due … [16:36]

And [even] before your time, [O Muhammad,] We never sent [as Our apostles] any but [mortal] men, whom We inspired: and if you have not [yet] realized this, ask the followers of [earlier] revelation, [16:43]

But We send [Our] message-bearers only as heralds of glad tidings and as warners… [18:56]

And, indeed, [O Muhammad,] We sent forth apostles before thy time; some of them We have mentioned to thee, and some of them We have not mentioned to thee. And it was not given to any apostle to bring forth a miracle other than by God's leave… [40:78]

Say thou, [O Prophet:] "I am but a mortal like you. It has been revealed to me that your God is the One God: go, then, straight towards Him and seek His forgiveness!" And woe unto those who ascribe divinity to aught beside Him. [41:6]

And how many a prophet did We send to people of olden times! [43:6]

## 1.8 Necessity of Faith

And give glad tidings to those who do good works that theirs shall be gardens under which waters flow. Whenever they are granted fruits there from they will say, "It is this that we were provided before." [2:25]

The Apostle, and the believers with him, believe in what has been given by their Lord. They all believe in Allah, and His angels, and His revelations, and His apostles, making no distinction between any of His apostles; and they say "We have heard, and we pay heed. Grant us forgiveness, O Lord". [2:285]

Those who say, "Our Lord! we believe, forgive us our sins, and save us from suffering through the fire". [3:16]

O you who believe! Respond to the call of Allah and the Apostle whenever he calls you to that which will give you life; and know that Allah intervenes between man and (the desires of) his heart, and that to Him you shall be gathered. [8:24]

And Moses said: "O my people! If you believe in Allah, place your trust in Him - if you have (truly) surrendered yourselves to Him!" [10:84]

Except those who repent and attain to faith and do righteous deeds: for it is they who will enter paradise and will not be wronged in any way. [19:60]

For those who deny the truth there is severe suffering, just as for those who believe and do righteous deeds there is forgiveness, and a great reward. [35:7]

## 1.9 The Real and Other Realities

Allah has sent the book in the truth and all those who dispute it are...in the wrong. [2:176]

O you who believe be conscious of Allah with all that is due to Him, and do not allow death to overtake you before submitting yourselves unto Him. [3:102]

And to Allah belongs all that is in the heavens and all that is on earth; and all things go back to (source) Allah. [3:109]

And obey Allah and the Apostle, so that you might be graced with mercy. [3:132]

Hence, place your trust in Allah (alone) - for, behold, that in which you believe is truth self-evident. [27:79]

He it is who has created the heavens and the earth in accordance with (an inner) truth. He causes the night to flow into the day; and causes the day to flow into the night; and He has made the sun and the moon subservient (to His laws), each running its course for a term set (by Him). Is not He the Almighty, the All-Forgiving? [39:5]

## 1.10 Submission to Truth

All that is with you is bound to come to an end, whereas that which is with Allah is everlasting. And most certainly shall We grant those who are patient (in adversity) their reward in accordance with the best that they did. [16:96]

... we have come to believe in our Lord, (hoping) that He may forgive us our faults... for Allah is the best, and the One who is truly abiding. [20:73]

Did you, then, think that We created you in mere idle play, and that you would not return to Us? Allah is sublimely exalted, the Ultimate Sovereign, the Ultimate truth:... [23:115-118]

And whatever you are given (now) is but for the (temporary) enjoyment of life in this world, and for its embellishment - whereas that which is with Allah is (much) better and remains forever. Will you, then, not use your reason? [28:60]

... the life of this world is nothing but amusement and a play - whereas, the life in the hereafter is indeed the only (true) life: if they knew this! [29:64]

Do they not reflect deeply about themselves? Allah has not created the heavens and the earth and all that is between them without truth and a term set and yet, there are many people who deny that they are destined to meet their Lord. [30:8]

And the face of your Lord full of majesty and glory will remain forever. [55:27]

Know (O men) that the life of this world is but a play and amusement, and a show, and boastful vying with one another... Its parable is that of (life-giving) rain: the herbage which it causes to grow delights the tillers of the soil; but then it withers, and you see it turn yellow; and it crumbles into dust... [57:20]

## 1.11 Natural Illusions

For those who persevere in doing good there is the ultimate good in store, and even more. No darkness or humiliation will overshadow their faces (on Resurrection Day): it is they who are destined for paradise, forever. [10:26]

He answered: "No, you throw (first)."... Their ropes and their sticks by their magic appeared to him as though they moved fast...[20:66]

But as for those who are denying the truth, their deeds are like a mirage in the desert, which the thirsty one supposes to be water - until, when he approaches it, he finds that it was nothing... [24:39]

And We send down from the skies water rich in blessings, and cause thereby gardens, and fields of grain that are reaped. [50:9]

All that lives upon it (earth) is bound to pass away: but forever will abide your Lord's face, full of majesty and glory. [55:26-27]

And the mountains will vanish as if they had been a mirage. [78:20]

But no, (O men,) you prefer the life of this world, although the life to come is better and more enduring. [87:16-17]

## 1.12 Ever-Present Perfection

All praise is due to Allah alone, the Lord of all the worlds. [1:2]

Allah - there is no deity save Him, the Ever-Living, Lord and protector of all that exists. Neither slumber nor sleep overtakes Him. His is all that is in the heavens and all that is on earth. Who is there that could intercede with Him, unless it be by His leave? He knows what happens to them in this world and in the hereafter, whereas they cannot attain to His knowledge except that which He wills. His power encompasses the heavens and the earth, and their preservation does not weary Him. Moreover, He alone is truly exalted, tremendous. [2:255]

Granting wisdom to whom He wills: and whoever is granted wisdom has indeed been granted great wealth. However, none remembers this except those with insight. [2:269]

(This is) the truth from your Lord; be not, among the doubters! [3:60]

And the life of this world is but a play and amusement; and the life in the hereafter is by far the better for all who are conscious of Allah. Will you not, then, use your reason? [6:32]

And your Lord alone is self-sufficient, limitless in His grace. If He so wills, He may put an end to you and in your place make whoever He wills to succeed you...[6:133]

All things does our Lord embrace within His knowledge; in Allah do we place our trust. O our Lord! Judge between us and our people in truth - for You are the best of all to open it up! [7:89]

Allah knows what any female bears (in her womb), and by how much the wombs may fall short (in gestation)... for with Him everything is (created) in accordance to an appropriate measure. [13:8]

Blessed is He in whose hand all dominion rests, and He has the power to will anything. He has created death and life to test which of you is best in deeds... [67:1-2]

Surely, We create man in the best stature (mould); [95:4]

## 1.13 The Qur'an Reveals Itself

And those who have no knowledge say, "Why does Allah not speak to us, nor is a (miraculous) sign shown to us?" ... We have made all the signs manifest to people who are endowed with inner certainty. [2:118]

It is He who has sent down to you the book, containing messages that are clear - and these are the essence of the book - as well as others that are allegorical. Now those whose hearts have deviated from the truth they follow what is confusing... those who are deeply rooted in knowledge say: "We believe in it; the whole book..." [3:7]

Surely, We have sent it down as an Arabic Qur'an, so that you might encompass it with your reason. [12:2]

We sent down through this Qur'an all that gives health and is a grace to those who believe (in Us), and it only adds to the ruin of evildoers. [17:82]

Is it not enough for them that We have sent down to you the book to be conveyed to them? For, verily, in it is grace, and a reminder to people who will believe. [29:51]

Allah has sent down the best of all teachings in the shape of a book fully consistent within itself, repeating each statement (of truth) in various ways – the skins of those who are in awe of their Lord shiver, and then their skins and their hearts do soften at the remembrance of Allah... Such is Allah's guidance: He guides him that wills (to be guided) - whereas whom Allah lets go astray can never find any guide. [39:23]

An Arabic Qur'an (clear) and free of all deviousness, so that they might become conscious of Allah. [39:28]

Now if We had willed this Qur'an to be a discourse in a non-Arabic tongue, they would surely have said, "Why is it that its messages have not been spelled out clearly (in our language)? Say: "To all who believe, it is a guidance and a source of health; but as for those who do not believe, in their ears is deafness, and so it remains obscure to them, they are (like people) being called from a far away place. [41:44]

And then We sent Our apostles to follow in their footsteps; We sent Jesus, the son of Mary, whom we gave the Bible; and in the hearts of those who (truly) followed him We engendered compassion and mercy. However, as for monastic asceticism - We did not prescribe it. They invented it themselves out of a desire to please Allah... [57:27]

# Chapter 2
# God's Light

## 2.1 The Supreme Light

His power encompasses the heavens and the earth, and their preservation does not weary Him... [2:255]

Now there has come unto you from Allah a light, and a clear book. [5:15]

Surely, We revealed the Torah in which was guidance and light... [5:44]

And We sent Jesus, the son of Mary following in their footsteps, confirming the Torah that came before him. We gave him the Gospel containing guidance and light... [5:46]

Is someone who was dead and whom We brought to life, supplying him with a light by which to walk among people, the same as someone who is in utter darkness, unable to emerge from it? [6:122]

It is He who appointed the sun to give radiance, and the moon to give light, assigning it phases so you would know the number of years and the reckoning of time. Allah did not create these things except with truth... [10:5]

And horses, mules and donkeys both to ride and for adornment. And He creates what you do not know. [16:8]

This is because Allah is the Truth and because He gives life to the dead and because He has power over all things. [22:6]

Allah is the Light of the heavens and the earth. ... Allah guides unto His light whoever He wills; and Allah sets forth parables for mankind, since Allah is cognizant of all things. [24:35]

(1) Say: 'He is Allah, Absolute Oneness, Allah, the Everlasting Lord of all. He has not given birth and was not born. And no one is comparable to Him.' [112:1-4]

## 2.2 The Incomparable One

... wherever you turn, there is the face of Allah. Behold, Allah is the All-Encompassing, All Knowing. [2:115]

And your God is one God! There is no god but Him ... [2:163]

Allah, there is no god but Him, the Living, the Self-Sustaining. ... His power encompasses the heavens and the earth, and their preservation does not tire Him. Moreover, He alone is truly exalted, tremendous. [2:255]

Whatever is in the heavens and in the earth belongs to Allah. Allah encompasses all things. [4:126]

Believe, then, in Allah and His apostles, and do not say, "(Allah is) a trinity". Desist, it is better for you; Allah is only one God; far be it from His glory that He should have a son. Whatever is in the heavens and whatever is in the earth is His. And Allah suffices as a Guardian. [4:171]

Allah says, 'Do not take two gods. He is only One God. So of Me alone should you be afraid.' [16:51]

If there were in the heavens and earth other gods besides God, there would have been confusion in both, but limitless in His glory is Allah, enthroned in His awesome almightiness beyond what men may associate or define! [21:22]

Allah is the Light of the heavens and the earth. ... Allah guides unto His light whoever He wills; and Allah sets forth parables for mankind, since Allah is cognizant of all things. [24:35]

He has given you mates from amongst yourselves – and given mates to the livestock – to multiply you thereby: (but) there is nothing like Him, and He alone is the All-hearing, the All seeing. [42:11]

It is He who created the heavens and the earth in six periods. ... And He is with you wherever you may be ... [57:4]

He is Allah – there is no god but Him; the Knower of the unseen and the seen; He is the Beneficent, the Merciful. [59:22]

He is Allah – there is no god but Him, ... the One to whom all greatness belongs! Utterly remote is Allah, ... from anything to which men may ascribe a share in His divinity! He is Allah ... To Him belongs the Most Beautiful Names. Everything in the heavens and earth glorifies Him... [59:23-24]

## 2.3 Pervading Essence

It is He who has made the earth a resting place for you, and the sky as a canopy and sent down rain from the sky and brought forth there with fruit as a provision for you. Then, do not knowingly make others equal to Allah. [2:22]

No human vision can encompass Him, whereas He encompasses all human vision ... [6:103]

(Allah) says: "My chastisement afflicts whom I will - but My grace overspreads everything: and so I shall confer it on those who are conscious of Me and spend in charity, and who believe in Our messages (signs). [7:156]

Say: 'To whom does the earth belong, and everyone in it, if you have any knowledge?' [23:84]

They will say: 'Allah's'. Say: 'Will you not then mind?' [23:85]

On that day Allah will pay back to them in full their just reward, and they shall know that Allah is the evident Truth. [24:25]

The life of this world is nothing but a game and a diversion. The abode of the Next World – that is truly life if they only knew. [29:64]

And they will ask their skins, "Why did you bear witness against us?" (and) these will reply: "Allah, who gives speech to all things, has given speech to us (as well): for He has created you in the first instance - and unto Him you are (now) brought back. [41:21]

He is the First and the Last, and the Outward as well as the Inward: and He has full knowledge of everything. [57:3]

It is He who has created the heavens and the earth in six periods ... And He is with you wherever you are; and Allah sees what you do. [57:4]

When the earth quakes with her (last) mighty quaking, and the earth brings forth its burdens, and man cries out, "What is the matter with it?" on that Day she shall tell all her news, because your Lord has inspired her to do that! [99:1-5]

## 2.4 God's Names and Signposts

Verily, nothing on earth or in the heavens is hidden from Allah. [3:5]

To Allah belongs the Most Beautiful Names, so call on Him by them and abandon those who desecrate His Names ... [7:180]

Call Him God or call Him the All-Merciful, whichever you call upon, He has the best names. Do not utter your prayer with a very raised voice nor be silent with regard to it, seek a way between these. [17:110]

Thus it is, because Allah alone is the (Ultimate) Truth and that which they invoke besides Him is sheer falsehood ... [31:30]

And He provides for him in a manner beyond all expectation and for everyone who places his trust in Allah, He (alone) is enough for him ... [65:3]

## 2.5 Earth's Nursery

It is He who made the earth a couch for you, and the sky a dome... Do not, then, knowingly make others equal to Allah. [2:22]

His power encompasses the heavens and the earth, and their preservation does not tire Him... [2:255]

Verily, in the creation of the heavens and the earth, and in the succession of night and day, there are indeed signs for all who are endowed with insight. [3:190]

It is He who has created you out of clay, and then has decreed a term (for you)... And yet you still have doubts! [6:2]

And it is He who causes you to be (like) dead at night, ... and He brings you back to life each day in order that a term set (by Him) be fulfilled. Then to Him is your return, then He will inform you of what you were doing. [6:60]

We have established you firmly on the earth and granted you your livelihood in it. Yet, how seldom are you grateful! [7:10]

Both creation and command belong to Him. Blessed be Allah, the Lord of all the worlds. [7:54]

Clearly does He spell out these messages, so that you might be certain in your innermost that you are destined to meet your Lord. [13:2]

Everyone in heaven and earth prostrates to Allah willingly or unwillingly, as do their shadows in the morning and the evening. [13:15]

And certainly We sent Moses with Our Signs, saying: Bring forth your people from utter darkness into light and remind them of the days of Allah; most surely there are signs in this for every patient, grateful one. [14:5]

... a day with your Lord is like a thousand years of your reckoning. [22:47]

Allah did not create the heavens and the earth and everything between them except with truth and for a fixed term. Yet many people reject the meeting with their Lord. [30:8]

The Lord of the heavens and the earth and all that is between them, the Almighty, the All-Forgiving!" [38:66]

Tell all who believe that they should forgive those who do not believe in the coming of the Days of Allah, He will recompense people according to what they have earned. [45:14]

Certainly they think it to be far off, but We see it (in truth) near! [70:6-7]

## 2.6 God's Commands

... a paradise as vast as the heavens and the earth, (is) prepared for the God conscious (people). [3.133]

And they returned (from the battle) with Allah's blessings and bounty, without having been touched by evil ... [3.174]

... all who believe in Allah and the Last Day and do righteous deeds – will not be in fear or grief. [5:69]

Respond to the call of Allah ... whenever He calls you ... and know that Allah intervenes between man and his heart, and that you will be gathered to Him. [8:24]

Anyone who acts rightly, male or female, being a believer, ... We will recompense them according to the best of what they did. [16:97]

Call (mankind) unto your Lord's way with wisdom and fair preaching, and argue with them in the most kindly manner ... [16:125]

Seek the abode of the Next World with what Allah has given you, without forgetting your portion of this world. And do good as Allah has been good to you. God does not love those who do mischief. [28:77]

That is because they who deny the truth pursue falsehood, whereas they who believe follow the truth from their Lord. In this way Allah makes comparisons for mankind. [47:3]

... and Allah does not love any of those who act in a boastful manner. [57:23]

O you who believe! Turn to Allah with sincere repentance: it may well be that your Lord will efface from you your wrong deeds, and will admit you into gardens through which running waters flow ... [66:8]

By time (its movement)! Certainly, man is at loss except those who believe, and do righteous actions, and urge each other to the truth and urge each other to steadfastness. [103:1-3]

## 2.7 God's Prohibitions

And then, after that, your hearts hardened and became like rocks, or even harder, and indeed there are stones from which streams gush forth ... [2:74]

Allah does not forgive anything being associated with Him but He forgives whoever He wills for anything other than that ... [4:48]

And the Jews say, "Allah's hand is shackled!" It is their own hands that are tied up (mean); and they are rejected by their assertion. Nay, both His hands stretched out: He dispenses (bounty) as He wills ... many of them are more stubborn in their arrogance and denial of the truth ... [5:64]

Yet why did they not, when Our punishment came to them, humble themselves? But their hearts hardened and the Shaytaan made what they did fair-seeming to them. [6:43]

... Beautify yourselves for acts of worship, and eat and drink, but do not waste: verily, He does not love the wasteful! [7:31]

Corruption has appeared ... on account of what the hands of men have wrought, that He may make them taste a part of that which they have done, so that they may return. [30:41]

## 2.8 Mercy and Forgiveness

My mercy encompasses everything: and so I shall confer it on those who are conscious of Me and spend in charity, and who believe in Our messages. [7:156]

Mankind were once a single community, and only later did they begin to hold divergent views. And had it not been for a decree - that had already gone forth from your Lord, all their differences would have disappeared. [10:19]

Behold, your Lord is full of forgiveness for men despite all their evildoing, and verily your Lord is (also) severe in retribution! [13:6]

Your Lord knows you best; He will have mercy on you if He pleases, or He will chastise you if He pleases ... [17:54]

Your Lord is the Ever-Forgiving, the Possessor of Mercy. If He had taken them to task for what they have earned, He would have hastened their punishment ... [18:58]

... do not despair of the mercy of Allah. Truly Allah forgives all wrong actions. He is the Ever-Forgiving, the Most Merciful.' [39:53]

The forgiver of sins and accepter of repentance, severe in retribution, limitless in His bounty ... [40:3]

The people of Nuh and the parties after them rejected (the prophets) before them, and every nation purposed against their apostle to destroy him ... therefore I destroyed them; how was then My retribution! [40:5]

Those who avoid grave sins and shameful deeds even though they may sometimes stumble - behold, your Lord is abounding in forgiveness. He is fully aware of you ... (for) He knows best as to who is conscious of Him. [53:32]

## 2.9 Levels of Awareness

Remember your Lord much and glorify Him in the evening and after dawn.' [3:41]

And remember your Lord within yourself humbly and with awe ... Do not be one of the unaware. [7:205]

They desire to extinguish Allah's (guiding) light with their utterances: but Allah will not allow (this) ... [9:32]

Those Allah humiliates will have no one to honour them; surely Allah does whatever He wills. [22:18]

... and they who act unjustly shall know to what final place of turning they shall turn back. [26:227]

Verily, in the Apostle of Allah you have a good example for everyone who looks forward (with hope) to Allah and the Last Day, and remembers Allah unceasingly. [33:21]

And when they are reminded (of the truth); they refuse to take it to heart. [37:13]

As guidance and a reminder to the men of understanding. [40:54]

All that is in the heavens and on earth glorify Allah, for He alone is Almighty, Wise! His is the dominion over the heavens and the earth ... and He has the power over all things. [57:1-2]

All that is in the heavens and on earth glorifies Allah, the Sacred King for He alone is Almighty, Wise! [62:1]

Have we not expanded your breast, and taken off from you your burden which pressed heavily upon your back? And have We not raised your remembrance? [94:1-4]

When Allah's help comes, and victory, and you see people enter Allah's religion in hosts, then glorify your Lord's praise and ask His forgiveness. He is the Ever-Returning. [110:1-3]

## 2.10 Remembrance of God

All things does my Lord embrace within His knowledge; will you not, then remember this? [6:80]

... and no bearer of burdens shall be made to bear another's burden. And, in time, unto your Lord you all must return ... [6:164]

And keep up prayer ... surely good deeds take away evil deeds, this is a reminder to the mindful. [11:114]

(The angels say): "We do not descend other than by thy Lord's command: unto Him belongs all that lies open before us and all that is hidden and in between. And never does your Lord forget. [19:64]

Verily, I am Allah; there is no god but Me. Hence, worship Me alone, and be constant in prayer, so as to remember Me! [20:14]

O you who believe! Remember Allah with unceasing remembrance. [33:41]

And your Lord says: "Call unto Me, (and) I shall respond to you!" [40:60]

And continue reminding for, verily, such a reminder will profit the believers. [51:55]

## 2.11 Trust in God

O you who believe! Remain conscious of Allah, and seek to be close to Him ... [5:35]

... "All praise is due to Allah, who has guided us unto this; for we would certainly not have found the right path unless Allah had guided us!" ... [7:43]

... "Is all this true?" Say: "Yes, by my Lord! It is most certainly true, and you cannot escape it!" [10:53]

He who created me and guides me ... [26:78]

And when I fall ill, it is He who heals me ... [26:80]

It is Allah who has bestowed revelation (from on high), by truth, and sanctioning justice And for all that you know the last hour may well be near. [42:17]

And keep up the balance with equity and do not shortchange in measuring. [55:9]

And the life to come is better and more enduring. [87:17]

## 2.12 Fear and Love of God

... those who follow My guidance will feel no fear and will know no sorrow. [2:38]

... everyone who surrenders his whole being unto Allah...shall be in no fear, nor will they grieve. [2:112]

And We will most certainly try you ... But give glad tidings unto those who are patient in adversity. [2:155]

... but truly pious is he who believes in Allah, ... it is they that have proved themselves true, and it is they, who are conscious of Allah. [2:177]

O you who believe! If you ever abandon your faith, Allah will in time bring forth people whom He loves and who love Him ... who strive hard in Allah's cause, and do not fear to be censured by anyone who might censure them: such is Allah's favor, which He grants unto whom He wills ... [5:54]

... all who believe in Allah and the Last Day and do righteous deeds – they shall have no fear nor shall they grieve. [5:69]

... all who believe and live righteously - no fear need they have, and neither shall they grieve; [6:48]

... And call unto Him with fear and longing: verily, Allah's grace is close to the doers of good! [7:56]

(Allah) says: "My chastisement afflicts whom I will - but My grace overspreads everything: and so I shall confer it on those who are conscious of Me and spend in charity, and who believe in Our messages (signs). [7:156]

Now surely the friends of Allah— they shall have no fear nor shall they grieve. [10:62]

And for him who fears to stand before his Lord are two gardens. [55:46]

## 2.13 Unity of Actions and Attributes

And your God is one God! There is no god but Him; He is the Beneficent, the Merciful. [2:163]

To Allah belong the Most Beautiful Names, so call on Him by them and abandon those who desecrate His Names... [7:180]

Allah is the Creator of all things, and He is the One, the Supreme. [13:16]

Allah, there is no god but Him. The Most Beautiful Names are His. [20:8]

And He is with you wherever you may be; and Allah sees all that you do. [57:4]

He is Allah ... To Him belong the Most Beautiful Names. Everything in the heavens and earth glorifies Him. He is the Almighty, the All-Wise. [59:24]

Surely it is to your Lord that you will return. [96:8]

## 2.14 The Essential Reference

Deaf, dumb (and) blind, so they will not turn back. [2:18]

... and if you are at variance over any matter, refer it unto Allah and the Messenger, if you believe in Allah and the Last Day. This is the best (for you), and best in the end. [4:59]

Oh, verily, His alone is all judgment: and He is the swiftest of all reckoners! [6:62]

They will be offering excuses to you when you return to them, say: "Do not offer excuses ... Allah has already enlightened us about you. ... and then He will make you truly understand what you were doing (in life)." [9:94]

"Behold, Allah lets go astray him who wills, just as He guides to Himself all who turn to Him. [13:27]

'Call on Allah or call on the All-Merciful, whichever you call upon, the Most Beautiful Names are His.'... [17:110]

So We rescued him and his family – except for his wife. We ordained her to be one of those who stayed behind. [27:57]

Corruption has appeared ... as an outcome of what men have earned, and so He will let them taste (the evil of) some of their doings, so that they may return. [30:41]

## 2.15 Friends of God

Be not, then, weak at heart, or grieve: for you are bound to rise high if you are believers. [3:138]

Those who remember Allah when they stand, and when they sit, and when they lie down on the side, and reflect upon the creation of the heavens and the earth: "O our lord! You have not created this without meaning and purpose. Glory to you! Keep us safe, then, from the torment of the fire!" [3:191]

... call on Him fearing and hoping; surely the mercy of Allah is close to those who do good. [7:56]

Now surely the friends of Allah shall have no fear nor shall they grieve. [10:62]

... verily, good deeds drive away evil deeds: this is a reminder to all who bear (Allah) in mind. [11:114]

And Who, I hope, will forgive me my faults on Judgment Day! [26:82]

And, indeed, a dispenser of grace is He unto the believers. [33:43]

And they will say: "All praise is due to Allah, who has caused all sorrow to leave us ... [35:34]

Indeed he who has purified himself will have success, [87:14] And magnifies the name of his Lord and prays. [87:15]

# Chapter 3
# Creation

**Introduction**

Those who are patient in adversity, and true to their word, and devout, and who spend (in charity), and pray for forgiveness from their innermost hearts. [3:17]

"All things are from Allah." What is wrong with these people that they fail to understand what is said? [4:78]

Every self will taste death. We test you with both good and evil as a trial. And you will be returned to Us. [21:35]

**3.1 Emergence of the Universe**

For it is He who has brought into being gardens ... Eat of their fruit when ripe, and give (the poor) their due on harvest day. And do not waste: verily, He does not love the wasteful! [6:141]

Your Lord creates and chooses whatever He wills. The choice is not theirs. Glory be to Allah ... [28:68]

But as for those who strive hard in Our cause - We shall most certainly guide them onto paths that lead unto Us ... [29:69]

And it is He who creates (all life) in the first instance, and then brings it forth anew: and this is easy for Him, since His is the essence of all ... [30:27]

It is Allah who created the heavens with no support – you can see them – and cast firmly embedded mountains on the earth so that it would not move under you, and scattered about in it creatures of every kind. And We send down water from the sky and make every generous species grow in it. [31:10]

He who has created all things in the best possible way ... [32:7]

And We send down from the skies water rich in blessings, and cause thereby gardens to grow, and fields of grain. [50:9]

Did We not create you out of a humble fluid? [77:20]

Verily, We create man in the best mould. [95:4]

## 3.2 God's Universe

... When He decrees an affair, He only says to it, Be, and it is. [2:117]

Allah will not take you to task for oaths which you may have uttered without thought, but will take you to task for what your hearts have earned and Allah is much forgiving, forbearing. [2:225]

And they ask you to hasten on the punishment ... and surely a day with your Lord is as a thousand years of what you number. [22:47]

But as for those who strive hard in Our cause - We shall most certainly guide them onto paths that lead unto Us ... [29:69]

And they do not truly know the measure (immensity) of Allah (as due to Him) ... glorified is He, and sublimely exalted above anything to which they may ascribe a share in His divinity! [39:67]

His are the keys of the heavens and the earth: He grants abundance to whom He wills, or gives it in scant measure, unto whomever He wills ... [42:12]

And surely to our Lord we must return. [43:14]

And for him who fears to stand before his Lord are two gardens. [55:46]

## 3.3 God's Will and Purpose

It is lawful for you to go in unto your wives during the night preceding the (day's) fast ... and do not have contact with them while you keep to the mosques; these are the limits of Allah, so do not go near them. Thus Allah makes clear His messages unto mankind, so that they might remain conscious of Him. [2:187]

And if you fear a breach between a married couple, appoint two arbitrators, one from his family and the other from hers, if they both desire agreement, Allah will affect harmony between them ... [4:35]

We have made the Signs clear for people who have knowledge. [6:97]

Allah will not change the (good and natural) condition of people as long as they do not alter it by themselves ... [13:11]

Know that the life of this world is but a play and amusement ... In the Next World there is terrible punishment but also forgiveness from Allah... The life of this world is nothing but the enjoyment of delusion. [57:20]

... You see no fault in the creation of the Most Gracious ... Then turn your vision again and yet again: your vision will return to you dazzled and humbled. [67:3-4]

## 3.4 This and Other Realms

Allah said: "Down with you, one of you is an enemy to the other, on earth will be your abode and livelihood for a while. [7:24]

They will be offering excuses to you when you return to them, say: "Do not offer excuses ... Allah has already enlightened us about you. ... and then He will make you truly understand what you were doing (in life)." [9:94]

... said they (who had deeper insight): "Your Lord knows best how long you have been here. Let, then, one of you go with these silver coins to the town, ... and bring some provisions. But let him behave with great care and by no means make anyone aware of you: [18:19]

... then when guidance comes to you from Me, he who follows My guidance will not go astray, nor be distressed. [20:123]

The keys of the heavens and earth belong to Him. It is those who reject Allah's Signs who are the losers. [39:63]

The angels and the spirit ascend unto Him in a day (period) the length of which is (like) fifty thousand years. [70:4]

Surely, they see it (day of reckoning) as far away. But We see it quite near. [70:6-7]

Has man ever known a point of time when he was not something remembered? [76:1]

## 3.5 Naturally in Transition

"Our colour (attributes) is from Allah! And who could give a better colour (qualities) to life than Allah; it is He that we worship." [2:138]

And We will most certainly try you ... But give glad tidings unto those who are patient in adversity. [2:155]

Those who, when disaster strikes them, say, "Verily, unto Allah do we belong and, verily, unto Him we shall return." [2:156]

It was the month of Ramadan in which the Qur'an was revealed as a guidance for man and a self-evident proof of that guidance, and as the criterion by which to discern the true from the false. Hence, whoever of you sees this month shall fast throughout it; but he that is ill, or on a journey, (shall fast instead) number of other days ... [2:185]

... it may well be that you hate a thing which is good for you, and it may well be that you love a thing which bad for you: and Allah knows, whereas you do not know. [2:216]

... (Allah) says: "My chastisement afflicts whom I will - but My grace overspreads everything: and so I shall confer it on those who are conscious of Me and spend in charity, and who believe in Our messages (signs)." [7:156]

Allah grants abundant sustenance, for whom He wills or reduces for whom He wills, and they rejoice in the life of this world - even though, compared to the life to come, the life of this world is but a fleeting pleasure. [13:26]

He who created death and life to test which of you is best in action. He is the Almighty, the Ever-Forgiving. [67:2]

Yet, you still prefer the life of this world, when the hereafter is better and more lasting. [87:16-17]

And, behold, with every hardship there is ease: verily, with every hardship there comes ease! [94:5-6]

### 3.6 Substances and Energy

Look at their fruit when it comes to fruition and ripens! Certainly, in this are signs for those who believe! [6:99]

And ask them about that town which stood by the sea ... Thus did We try them by means of their (own) iniquitous doings. [7:163]

And He it is who has created the heavens and the earth in six periods; ... And if you say, "Certainly, you shall be raised up after death!" – those who deny the truth say, "This is nothing but an enchanting delusion. [11:7]

We send forth the pollinating winds and send down water from the sky and give it to you to drink. And it is not you who keep its stores. [15:22]

Do not those who disbelieve see that the heavens and the earth were closed up, but We have opened them; and We have made of water everything living ...? [21:30]

We said "O fire! Be coolness and peace for Abraham!" [21:69]

Allah is the Light of the heavens and the earth. ... Allah guides unto His light whoever He wills; and Allah sets forth parables for mankind, since Allah is Knower of all things. [24:35]

"Strike the ground with your foot and there will be cool water to wash with and to drink!" [38:42]

And they do not truly know the measure (immensity) of Allah (as due to Him) ... glorified is He, and sublimely exalted above anything to which they may ascribe a share in His divinity! [39:67]

## 3.7 Dualities and other Reflections

And Allah has ... provided for you sustenance out of the good things. Will men believe in falsehood and deny Allah's favours? [16:72]

He it is who has made the earth a cradle for you, and has made for you paths (of livelihood) ... [20:53]

Glory be to Him who created everything pairs: from what the earth produces and from themselves and from things unknown to them. [36:36]

And He it is who has created pairs of all things. And it is He who has provided for you ships and animals upon which you ride. [43:12]

And of everything We have created pairs that you may be mindful. [51:49]

And that He created pairs, the male and the female. [53:45]

Allah is He who has created seven heavens, and like them of the earth. Through them flows His will, so that you might come to know that Allah has the power to will anything, and that Allah encompasses all things with His knowledge. [65:12]

And We have created you in pairs. [78:8]

## 3.8 Angels, *Jinn* (invisible beings) and Demons

... certainly Allah is the enemy of all who deny the truth. [2:98]

... if you are patient in adversity and keep your duty ... your Lord will aid you with five thousand angels swooping down! [3:125]

We never send down angels except in accordance with the truth ... [15:8]

And to Allah prostrates every creature that is in the heavens and earth, and the angels too, and they are not proud. [16:49]

We said to the angels, "Prostrate yourselves before Adam" - whereupon they all prostrated themselves, except Iblis ... [17:61]

And you will see the angels surrounding the throne of (Allah's) power, glorifying their Lord with praise ... [39:75]

Or do those in whose hearts is disease think that Allah would never bring their moral failings to light? [47:29]

I only created the Jinn and man to worship Me. [51:56]

And He created the jinn from a flame of fire. [55:15]

## 3.9 Human Evolution

And We said: "O Adam, dwell you and your wife in this garden, and eat freely from it, both of you, whatever you may wish; but do not approach this one tree, for then you will be of the unjust. [2:35]

... then whoever is drawn away from the fire and brought into paradise will indeed have gained a triumph: for the life of this world is nothing but a provision of vanities. [3:185]

He (God) said "Down with you, some of you the enemies of another, having on earth an abode and livelihood for a while". [7:24]

And do not spread corruption on earth after it has been well ordered. And call upon Him with fear and hope, certainly, Allah's grace is ever near unto the doers of good! [7:56]

Whoever desires this world's life and its bounties ... they shall not be deprived of their just due therein: it is they who, in the life to come, shall have nothing but the fire ... and worthless all that they ever did! [11:15-16]

It is He who brings forth the living out of the dead, and brings forth the dead from the living ... and thus you shall be brought forth. [30:19]

And it is He who originates creation and reproduces it anew, and it is easy for Him and His are the most exalted attributes in the heavens and the earth ... [30:27[

It is He who creates you out of dust, and then out of a drop of sperm, ... and then, that you grow old - though some of you die earlier ... so that you might use your reason. [40:67]

## 3.10 Individuals and Groups

We prescribed for the children of Israel that if anyone kills a human being ... it is as though he had killed all mankind; whereas, if anyone saves a life, it is as though he had saved the lives of all mankind ... [5:32]

And if Allah had willed, He could surely have made you all one single community, but in order to test you by means of what He has entrusted you with. Vie, then, with one another in doing good works, to Allah you will return; and then He will inform you in what you differed. [5:48]

And who could be more wicked than he who attributes lies regarding God, these will be brought before their Lord ... Surely the curse of Allah is on the unjust. [11:18]

... certainly, all falsehood is bound to vanish!" [17:81]

Surely, We made everything on earth an adornment for it so that We may try which of them are best in conduct. [18:7]

Glory be to Him who created all the pairs: from what the earth produces and from themselves and from things unknown to them. [36:36]

I only created jinn and man to worship Me. [51:56]

## 3.11 In a Direction

Lost indeed are they who reject meeting God ... and they shall bear on their backs the burden of their sins... [6:31]

And so We shall forsake them today as they were oblivious to the coming of this Day (of Judgment), and as they denied Our messages. [7:51]

Verily, as for those who do not believe that they are destined to meet Us, but content themselves with the life of this world and do not look beyond it, and are heedless of Our messages – [10:7]

These are they who disbelieve in the communications of their Lord and His meeting, so their deeds become null ... [18:105]

Allah is the Light of the heavens and the earth. ... Allah guides unto His light whoever He wills; and Allah sets forth parables for mankind, since Allah is cognizant of all things. [24:35]

Whoever hopes to meet Allah, the term appointed by Allah will then most surely come ... [29:5]

And it is He who creates (all life) in the first instance, and then brings it forth anew: and this is easy for Him, since His is the essence of all ... [30:27]

And paradise will be brought near to the God conscious, and will not be far away. [50:31]

Verily, the Allah-conscious will find themselves in gardens and in bliss. [52:17]

On Him depend all creatures in the heavens and on earth ... [55:29]

Surely they think it to be far off ... [70:6]

Hence, leave them to indulge in idle talk and play until they face that Day of theirs which they have been promised. [70:42]

No, but (most of) you love this fleeting life. [75:20]

## 3.12 Capacity and Readiness

But there are among them who say, "O our Lord! Grant us good in this world and good in the life to come, and keep us safe from suffering through the fire". [2:201]

We do not impose on any soul a duty except to the extent of its ability; and when you speak, then be just though it be a relative, and fulfil Allah's covenant; this He has enjoined you with that you may be mindful. [6:152]

... verily, good deeds drive away evil deeds: this is a reminder to all who bear (Allah) in mind. [11:114]

There is no community which We will not destroy before the Day of Resurrection, or chastise with severe suffering: all this is laid down in Our book (of decrees). [17:58]

... and pay no heed to any whose heart We have rendered unmindful of our remembrance because he had followed his low desires and whose life has transgressed all bounds. [18:28]

And there is nothing concealed in the heaven and the earth but it is in a clear book. [27:75]

O you who believe! Obey God and obey His Messenger, and do not make your deeds of no effect! [47:33]

There is indeed a reminder in this for everyone whose heart is wide-awake, and lends ear with a conscious mind. [50:37]

Surely, We have created everything in due measure. [54:49]

And, verily, this is a reminder to all those who are God conscious! [69:48]

## 3.13 Orbits and Cycles Within a Whole

And it is He Who created the night and the day and the sun and the moon; all travel along swiftly in their orbits. [21:33]

And neither may the sun overtake the moon, nor can the night outstrip the day, since all of them float in orbits. [36:40]

... and He has made the sun and the moon subservient, each running its course for a term set. Is He not the Almighty, the All-Forgiving? [39:5]

... warn (them) of the Day of the Gathering, which is beyond all doubt: (the Day when) some shall find themselves in paradise, and some in the blazing flame. [42:7]

The All-Merciful. Has imparted this Qur'an. He has created humankind; and taught him eloquent speech. [55:1-4]

He who has created seven heavens in harmony with one another, no fault will thou see in the creation of the All-Merciful ... [67:3]

No! I call to witness the accusing soul (voice of man's own conscience). [75:2]

You are bound to move; onward from stage to stage. [84:19]

I swear by the night when it draws a veil, And the day when it shines in brightness, And the creating of the male and the female,

Your striving is most surely (directed to) various (ends). Then as for him who gives away and is conscious of Allah, and accepts the best, We will facilitate for him the easy end. And as for him who is niggardly and considers himself free from need (of Allah), and rejects the best, We will facilitate for him the difficult end. And his wealth will not avail him when he perishes. Surely Ours it is to show the way, And most surely Ours is the hereafter and the former. Therefore I warn you of the fire that flames: None shall enter it but the most unhappy, who gives the lie (to the truth) and turns (his) back. And away from it shall be kept the one who is truly conscious of Allah, who gives away his wealth, purifying himself'; and no one has with him any boon for which he should be rewarded, Except the seeking of the pleasure of his Lord, the Most High. And he shall soon be well-pleased. [92:1-21]

# Chapter 4
## Adam and Human Nature

### 4.1 Adam in Paradise

And when your Lord said to the angels: "Behold, I am about to establish upon earth a steward. They said: "Will you place on it one who will spread corruption and shed blood - whereas we glorify you with praise and proclaim your purity?" He said: "I know that which you do not know." And He taught Adam all the names then He presented them to the angels and said: "Tell Me the names of these (things), if you are right." They replied: "Glory be to you, we have no knowledge except what you have taught us." You are the All-Knowing, Truly Wise." He said: "O Adam, inform them of the names of these things." And as soon as he had informed them of their names, He said: "Did I not tell you that I alone know all the realities of the heavens and the earth, and know all that you bring into the open and all that you conceal?" And when We told the angels, "Prostrate yourselves before Adam!" - they all prostrated themselves, except Iblis, who refused and was proud and was one of those who deny the truth. And We said: "O Adam, you and your wife dwell in this garden, and eat freely, both of you, whatever you may wish; but do not approach this one tree, lest you become wrongdoers." [2:30-35]

O Mankind! Keep your duty to your Lord, who has created from a single living being, and out of it created its mate, from these two, spread abroad a multitude of men and women. And perform your duty to Allah, by whom you demand from one another, and of family. Allah is ever watchful over you! [4:1]

Allah said: "Down with you, enemies to each other, on earth will be your home and livelihood for a while. [7:24]

And when We said to the angels, "Prostrate yourselves before Adam" - so they all prostrated themselves, except Iblis, he said: "Shall I prostrate myself before one whom you have created out of clay?" [17:61]

And when We told the angels, "Prostrate yourselves before Adam," they all prostrated themselves, except Iblis: he was one of the Jinn, who transgressed the commandment of his Lord. Will you, then, take him and his associates as friends instead of Me, although they are your enemies? How evil is this exchange. [18:50]

And indeed We gave Our commandment to Adam before; but he forgot, and We found no firmness of resolve in him. [20:115]

... when We told the angels, "Prostrate yourselves before Adam!" - they all prostrated themselves, except Iblis, who refused. [20:116]

We said: "O Adam! this is an enemy to you and your wife: so let him not drive the two of you out of this garden and render you unhappy. Surely, it is provided for you that you will not hunger here or feel naked, and that you shall not thirst or suffer from the heat of the sun." [20:117-119]

But Satan whispered to him, "O Adam! Shall I lead you to the tree of eternal life; and to a kingdom that will never decay?" [20:120]

## 4.2 Descent and Ascent of Adam

And when your Lord said to the angels: "Behold, I am about to establish upon earth a steward. They said: "Will you place on it one who will spread corruption and shed blood - whereas we glorify you with praise and proclaim your purity?" He Said: "I know that which you do not know." And He taught Adam all the names then He presented them to the angels and said: "Tell Me the names of these (things), if you are right." They replied: "Glory be to you, we have no knowledge except what you have taught us." You are the All-Knowing, Truly Wise." He said: "O Adam, inform them of the names of these things." And as soon as he had informed them of their names, He said: "Did I not tell you that I alone know all the realities of the heavens and the earth, and know all that you bring into the open and all that you conceal?" And when We told the angels, "Prostrate yourselves before Adam!" - they all prostrated themselves, except Iblis, who refused and was proud and was one of those who deny the truth. [2:30-34]

"You make the night to enter the day, and you make the day enter the night. And you bring the living out of the dead, and you bring the dead out of the living. And you give sustenance to whom you please, without measure." [3:27]

Are the unbelievers not aware that the heavens and the earth were one single entity, which We then split? And We made out of water every living thing? Will they not then believe? [21-30]

O Men! If you are in doubt as to the resurrection, remember, certainly, We have created you out of dust, then out of a drop of sperm, then out of a germ-cell, then out of an embryonic lump complete in itself and yet incomplete, so that We might make your origin clear to you. And whatever We will We cause to rest in the womb for a set term, and then We bring you forth as infants and give you growth so that you attain to maturity, among you are those who die (in childhood), just as many a one of you is reduced in old age to a most abject state, ceasing to know anything of what he once knew so well. You can see the earth dry and lifeless - and (suddenly,) when We send down waters upon it, it stirs and swells and brings forth every kind of beautiful growth! [22:5]

Who makes excellent everything He creates. Thus, He begins the creation of man out of clay. [32-7]

O man – Certainly you are striving toward your Lord, a striving which you will meet in His presence! [84:6]

Surely, We create man in the best form. [95-4]

## 4.3 Acting Stewardship

And when your Lord said to the angels: "Behold, I am about to establish upon earth a steward. They said: "Will you place on it that which will spread corruption and shed blood - whereas we only glorify you, and praise your holiness?" (Allah) answered: "Certainly, I know that which you do not." [2:30]

And compete with one another to attain your Lord's forgiveness and a paradise as vast as the heavens and the earth, which has been prepared for the God conscious [3:133]

For them there is the glad tiding (of happiness) in the life of this world and in the life to come; (and since) nothing could ever alter (the outcome of) Allah's promises, this is the supreme triumph! [10:64]

As for those men or woman - who does righteous deeds, and believe – those shall We most certainly cause to live a good life and most certainly shall We grant them their reward in accordance with the best that they did. [16:97]

Have they not travelled through the earth, allowing their hearts to gain wisdom, and allowing their ears to hear? Yet, verily, it is not eyes that have become blind - but the hearts that are in their breasts! [22:46]

If He so wills, He can make you go (disappear) and bring forth new creation ... [35:16]

... so that they might think for themselves; (and We have revealed it) in the Arabic tongue, free of all deviousness, so that they might become conscious of Allah.[39:7]

(And We said:) "O David! Behold, We have made you a prophet and vicegerent on earth: judge, then, between men with justice, and do not follow vain desire, lest it lead you astray from the path of Allah." [39:28]

O you who believe! Turn to Allah in sincere repentance: it may well be that your Lord will remove from you your bad deeds, and will admit you into gardens through which running waters flow, on a Day which Allah will not shame the Prophet and those who believe with him ... [66:8]

## 4.4 Human Composition

"And yet, I am not trying to absolve myself: for, indeed, man's inner self does incite (him) to evil, and only they upon whom my Lord bestows His grace are saved." [12:53]

"And when I have formed him fully and breathed into him of My spirit, fall down before him in prostration!" [15:29]

And they will ask you about the nature of divine inspiration. Say: "This inspiration comes at my Lord's command; and you cannot understand its nature, O men, since you have been granted very little of (real) knowledge." [17:85]

Consider the soul and Him who perfected it, and inspired it with consciousness of right and wrong, he is indeed successful who causes it to grow, and he is indeed a failure who stunts its growth. [91:7-10]

## 4.5 Sublime and Ridiculous

Fighting is prescribed for you, even though it be hateful to you; but it may well be that you hate a thing that is good for you, and love a thing that is bad for you: and Allah knows, whereas you do not know. [2:216]

And the unbelievers plotted (against Jesus); but Allah brought their scheming to nothing: for Allah is above all schemers. [3:54]

And it is in this way that We cause the great ones in every land to become its greatest evildoers, there to weave their schemes: yet it is only against themselves that they scheme - and they do not perceive it. [6:123]

Can they ever feel secure from Allah's devising? But none feels secure from Allah's devising save people who are lost. [7:99]

Those who lived before devised indeed - but all devising is that of Allah, who knows what each human being earns: and the disbelievers will come to know for whom is the good end. [13:42]

And they have indeed devised their plan - and all their devising is within Allah's knowledge. Even though their devising could move mountains. [14:46]

And it is a descent from the Lord of the worlds. The faithful spirit has brought it. Upon your heart so that you are from amongst the warners. [26: 191-193]

Let him who has means spend in accordance with his means; and let him whose means of subsistence is small spend in accordance with what Allah has given him: Allah does not burden any human being with more than He has given him - and it may well be that Allah will grant ease after hardship. [65:7]

And when they are told, "Bow down (before Allah)", they do not bow down. [77:48]

Consider the soul and Him who perfected it, and inspired it with consciousness of right and wrong,, he is indeed successful who causes it to grow, and he is indeed a failure who stunts its growth. [91:7-10]

Verily, those who disbelieve among the followers of earlier revelation or from among those who ascribe divinity to other than Allah - will find themselves in the fire of hell, therein to abide: they are the worst of all creatures. [98:6]

## 4.6 Mind, Body and Soul

And so, the parable of those who disbelieve is that of the beast which hears the shepherd's cry, and hears in it nothing but the sound of a voice and a call. They are deaf, dumb and blind: for they do not use their reason. [2:171]

And most certainly have We destined for hell many of the Jinn and mankind whose hearts failed to grasp the truth, and eyes with which they failed to see, and ears with which they failed to hear. They are like cattle - no, they are even less conscious of the right way, it is they who are heedless! [7:179]

And never concern yourself with that of which you have no knowledge: certainly your hearing, sight and heart - all of them - will be called to account for it (on Judgment Day)! [17:36]

Those whose eyes had been veiled from my reminder, who were incapable of listening (to the voice of truth)! [18:101]

Have they not travelled through the earth, allowing their hearts to gain wisdom, and allowing their ears to hear? Yet, verily, it is not eyes that have become blind - but the hearts that are in their breasts! [22:46]

We inspired him (Nuh): "Build, under Our eyes and according to Our inspiration, the ark. And when Our judgment comes to pass, and waters gush forth over the earth, place on board one pair of each kind as well as your family - except those on whom sentence has already been passed - and do not appeal to Me on behalf of those who are unbelievers - certainly, they are destined to be drowned! [23:27]

On the Day when their own tongues, hands and feet will bear witness against them by (recalling) all that they did! [24:24]

Just as you cannot not lead the blind (of heart) out of their error: none can you make to hear except those who believe in Our messages, and surrender themselves to Us. [30:53]

And when I have formed him fully and breathed My spirit into him, bow down before him in prostration. [38:72] O man – Certainly you are striving toward your Lord a hard striving until you meet Him! [84:6]

## 4.7 Author of Fate

And We gave him Isaac and Jacob; and We guided each of them as We had guided Noah before. And out of his offspring, We gave Prophethood to David, Solomon, Job, Joseph, Moses, and Aaron: for thus do We reward the doers of good. [6:84]

Whoever shall come (before Allah) with a good deed will gain ten times its equivalent; but whoever shall come with an evil deed will be recompensed with no more than the equivalent; and none shall be wronged. [6:160]

Hell will be their abode and their covering, thus do We recompense the evildoers. [7:41]

And know that your worldly possessions and your children are but a trial and a temptation, and that with Allah, there is a tremendous reward. [8:28]

(And all shall be judged on that Day,) so that Allah may recompense every human being for all that he has earned, certainly, Allah is swift in reckoning! [14:51]

All that is with you is bound to come to an end, whereas that which is with Allah is everlasting. And most certainly shall We grant those who are patient (in adversity) their reward in accordance with the best that they did. [16:96]

Every human being is bound to taste death; and We test all through the bad and the good (things of life): and to Us you will return. But whenever the unbelievers consider you, they make a mockery of you, (saying) "Is this the one who speaks (so contemptuously) of your Gods?" [21:35-36]

Do men think that by merely saying, "We believe", they will be left to themselves, and will not be put to a test? [29:2]

If you deny the truth (being ungrateful) - certainly, Allah has no need of you; none the less, He does not approve of ingratitude in His servants: whereas, if you show gratitude, He approves it in you. And no carrier of burdens shall be made to bear another's burden. In time, to your Lord you all will return, He will then tell you what you were doing, certainly, He has full knowledge of what is in the hearts (of men). [39:7]

On that Day will every human being be recompensed for what he has earned: no wrong (will be done) on that Day: certainly, Allah is swift in reckoning! [40:17]

Tell those who believe that they should pardon those who do not hope in the coming of the Days of Allah, (since it is) for Him (alone) to recompense people for whatever they may have earned. [45:14]

## 4.8 Punishment and Reward

And We cause the clouds to comfort you with their shade, and sent down to you manna and quails, (saying), "Partake of the good things which We have provided sustenance." And (all their sinning) does no harm to Us - but (only) against their own selves. [2:57]

Then, after grief, He sent down upon you a sense of security, slumber (an inner calm) which embraced some of you, the others, who cared mainly for themselves, entertained wrong thoughts about Allah - thoughts of pagan ignorance - saying, "Did we, then, have any power of decision (in this matter)?" [3:154]

And when those who believe in Our messages come to you, say: "Peace be upon you. Your Lord has willed upon Himself the law of grace and mercy - so that if any of you does a bad deed out of ignorance, and thereafter repents and lives righteously, He is Forgiving, Merciful." [6:54]

Hence, those who deny Our messages, and the meeting of the hereafter – their actions are in vain, can they be rewarded except for what they do? [7:147]

"If you do good, you do good to yourselves; and if you do evil, you do it to yourselves." And so, when the second warning came, (We raised new enemies against you, and allowed them) to disgrace you utterly, and to enter the mosque as they had done before, and to destroy all that they had conquered with utter destruction. [17:7]

But as for him who believes and does good - he will have the ultimate good in the hereafter as a reward; and we shall make binding on him only that which is easy to fulfil. [18:88]

Corruption has appeared on land and sea as a consequence of man's actions, that He may let them taste its effect, so that they might return (to the right way). [30:41]

But (remember that an attempt at) punishing evil may, too, become an evil: hence, whoever pardons (his foe) and makes peace, his reward rests with Allah - for, certainly, He does not love evildoers. [42:40]

O man – you have, certainly been striving towards your Lord in hard striving - then you will meet Him! [84:6]

## 4.9 Vices of the Self

And, after all this, your hearts hardened and became like stones, or even harder; and surely there are stones from which streams gush forth; there are some from which, when split, water flows; and there are some that fall down due to awe of Allah. And Allah is not unmindful of what you do! [2:74]

Alluring to man is the enjoyment of worldly desires through women, and children, and heaped-up treasures of gold and silver, and horses of high distinction, and cattle, and land. All this may be enjoyed in the life of this world - but the best of all goals is with Allah. [3:14]

O Children of Adam! adorn yourselves for every act of worship, and eat and drink (freely), but do not waste: verily, He does not love the wasteful! [7:31]

Say: "My Lord has forbidden only shameful deeds, be they open or secret, and sin, and unjust oppression, and the associating with Allah, for which permission is not granted, and attributing to Allah that which you have no knowledge of." [7:33]

And certainly have We destined for hell many of the jinn and humans whose hearts failed to grasp the truth, whose eyes failed to see, and whose ears failed to hear. They are like cattle - no, they are more astray, it is they who are heedless! [7:179]

And at sea, whenever you are in danger, all whom you call upon fail you, except Him: but as soon as you are safe ashore, you turn away – for man is ungrateful! [17:67]

And there are many who worship Allah on the border-line (of faith): if good befalls him, he is satisfied with Him; but if a trial afflicts him, he turns away, losing this world and the hereafter: this, indeed, is a loss beyond compare. [22:11]

And do not turn away from people in (false) pride, and do not walk arrogantly on earth: for, certainly, Allah does not love anyone who,(out of self conceit) acts in a boastful manner. [31:18]

Certainly, man is born with a restless disposition. Whenever misfortune touches him, he is filled with self-pity; and whenever good fortune comes to him, he selfishly withholds it (from others). Not so, those who consciously turn towards Allah in prayer; who persevere in their prayer; and in whose wealth there is an acknowledged right, for the beggar and destitute; and who believe in the day of judgment; and who stand in awe of their Lord's chastisement for, certainly, none can ever feel secure from their Lord's chastisement. [70:19-28]

## 4.10 Virtues of the Soul

O you who believe! Seek aid in steadfast patience and prayer: for, certainly, Allah is with those who are patient in adversity. [2:153]

O Children of Adam! Indeed, We have brought upon you (the knowledge of) making garments to cover your nakedness, and as a thing of beauty: but the garment of God consciousness is the best. Herein lies a message (from Allah), so that man might take it to heart. [7:26]

It is they, who are truly believers! They shall have grades of dignity in their Lord's sight, and forgiveness of sins, and a most excellent sustenance. [8:4]

And whenever they spend anything (for the sake of Allah), be it little or much, and whenever they move on earth (in Allah's cause) - it is recorded in their favour, and Allah will grant them the best reward for all that they have been doing. [9:121]

Save those who are patient in adversity and do righteous deeds: it is they whom forgiveness of sins awaits, and a great reward. [11:11]

It is they who compete with each other in doing good works, and it is they who outrun (all others) in attaining to them! [23:61]

Trustworthy divine spirit (Gabriel) has alighted with it from on high. [26:193]

He it is who has created the heavens and the earth in six days, and established Himself on the throne (of His Almightiness) ... [57:4]

Although the life to come is better and more enduring. [87:17]

## 4.11 The Wholesome Heart

In their hearts is disease, and so Allah lets their disease increase; and grievous suffering awaits them because of their persistent lying. [2:10]

And, after all this, your hearts hardened and became like stones, or even harder; and surely there are stones from which streams gush forth; there are some from which, when split, water flows; and there are some that fall down due to awe of Allah. And Allah is not unmindful of what you do! [2:74]

And Allah inspired this only as a glad tiding for you, and that your hearts should be at rest - help comes only from Allah, the Almighty, Wise. [3:126]

Believers are they whose hearts tremble with awe whenever Allah is mentioned, and whose faith is strengthened whenever His messages are conveyed to them; and who place their trust in their Lord. [8:2]

O Prophet, say to the captives who are in your hands: "If Allah finds any good in your hearts, He will give you something better than all that has been taken from you, and will forgive you your sins: for Allah is All-Forgiving, Merciful." [8:70]

Those who believe, and whose hearts find their rest in the remembrance of Allah - for, verily, in the remembrance of Allah do hearts find rest. [13:28]

Have they not travelled through the earth, allowing their hearts to gain wisdom, and allowing their ears to hear? Certainly, it is not the eyes that are blind - but the hearts that are in their breasts! [22:46]

Only he (will be happy) who comes before Allah with a wholesome heart. [26:89]

... an aching void grew up in the heart of the mother of Moses, and she would indeed have disclosed all about him had We not endowed her heart with enough strength to keep her faith alive. [28:10]

And know that Allah's Apostle is among you: were he to comply with your inclinations in each and every case, you would be bound to come to harm. But as it is, Allah has caused faith to be dear to you, and has given it beauty in your hearts, and has made hateful to you all denial of the truth, and all injustice, and all rebellion (against what is good). Such indeed are they who follow the right course [49:7]

## 4.12 To Witness and Transcend

But when you are greeted with a greeting (of peace), answer with an even better greeting, or (at least) with its like. Certainly, Allah keeps count of all things. [4:86]

O you who believe! Respond to the call of Allah and the Apostle whenever he calls you to that which will give you life; and know that Allah intervenes between man and (the desires of) his heart, and that to Him you shall be gathered. [8:24]

For them there is the glad tidings in the life of this world and in the hereafter; nothing could ever alter (the outcome of) Allah's decrees (ways), this is the supreme achievement! [10:64]

Those who believe, and whose hearts find rest in the remembrance of Allah - for, certainly, in the remembrance of Allah do hearts find rest.; [13:28]

As for anyone - be it man or woman - who does righteous deeds, and is a believer, We will certainly cause them to live a good life and certainly, We shall grant them their reward in accordance with the best that they did. [16:97]

And to (the people of) Madyan (We sent) their brother Shu'ayb, who said: "O my people! Worship Allah (alone), and look forward to the Last Day, and do not act wickedly on earth by spreading corruption!" [29:36]

(And as for thee,) O Prophet - certainly, We have sent you as a witness and as a bearer of glad tidings and a warner. [33:45]

... for Allah (alone) knows what is in your hearts - and Allah is indeed All-Knowing, Forbearing. [33:51]

The living and the dead (of heart) are not equal. Certainly, (O Muhammad) Allah can make hear whomever He wills, whereas you cannot make to hear such as are (dead of heart, like the dead) in their graves: [35:22]

But Allah's is the Kingdom over the heavens and the earth: He forgives whomever He wills, and imposes suffering on whomever He wills - and He is indeed All-Forgiving, Merciful. [48:14]

You cannot find people who (truly) believe in Allah and the Last Day and (at the same time) love anyone who contends against Allah and His Apostle - even though they be their fathers, or their sons, or their brothers, or (others of) their family. (As for the true believers,) it is they in whose hearts He has given faith, and whom He has strengthened with inspiration from Himself, and whom (in time) He will admit into gardens through which running waters flow, to abide therein. Well-pleased is Allah with them, and well pleased are they with Him. They are Allah's party: certainly, it is the party of Allah, who shall attain to a successful state! [58:22]

In them, indeed, you have a good example for everyone who looks forward (with hope and awe) to Allah and the Last Day. And if any turns away, (let him know that) Allah is truly self-sufficient, the One to whom all praise is due." [60:6]

## 4.13 Decree and Destiny

He is the Originator of the heavens and the earth: and when He wills a thing to be, He but says to it, "Be" - and it is. [2:117]

It is not Allah's will (O you who disbelieve) to abandon the believers to your way of life: (and) to that end He will set apart the bad from the good. And it is not Allah's will to give you insight into that which is beyond the reach of human perception: but (to that end) Allah elects whomsoever He wills from among His apostles. Believe, then, in Allah and His apostles; for if you believe and are conscious of Him, a magnificent reward awaits you. [3:179]

Certainly, Allah does not wrong (anyone) by as much as an atom's weight; and if there be a good deed, He will multiply it, and will give out of His grace a mighty reward. [4:40]

And He it is who has created the heavens and the earth in accordance with (an inner) truth ... [6:73]

Postponing (procrastination) of the sacred months is an addition of disbelieve, a means by which unbelievers are led astray. They declare this postponement to be permissible in one year and forbidden in another, in order to conform (outwardly) to the number of months which Allah has made sacred: and thus they make permissible what Allah has forbidden. The evil of their own doings seems good to them, Allah does not grace with His guidance people who refuse to acknowledge the truth. [9:37]

It does not behove the people of the (Prophet's) City and the Bedouin (who live) around them to hold back from following Allah's Apostle, or to care for their own selves more than for him - for, whenever they suffer from thirst or weariness or hunger in Allah's cause, and whenever they take any step which confounds the unbelievers, and whenever there comes to them from the enemy whatever may be destined for them - a good deed is recorded in their favour. Certainly, Allah does not fail to reward the doers of good! [9:120]

But as for those who have done evil deeds - the recompense of an evil, deed shall be its like - and since they will have none to defend them against Allah - ignominy will overshadow them as though their faces were veiled by the night's own darkness: it is they who are destined for the fire, to abide therein. [10:27]

And be constant in praying at the beginning and the end of the day, as well as during the early parts of the night: for, certainly, good deeds drive away evil deeds: this is a reminder to all who bear (Allah) in mind. [11:114]

But those who have attained to faith and have always been conscious of Us, a reward in the life to come is a far greater reward. [12:57]

... certainly, Allah will not change the (good and natural) condition of people as long as they do not alter it by themselves (through wrong action). And when Allah wills people to suffer evil (in consequence of their own evil deeds), there is none who could avert it: for they have none who could protect them from Him. [13:11]

Certainly, as for those who believe and do righteous deeds - Certainly, We do not fail to reward any who persevere in doing good. [18:30]

"Therefore, whoever looks forward (with hope and awe) to meeting his Lord (on Judgment Day), let him do righteous deeds, and let him not ascribe to anyone or anything a share in the worship due to his Lord !" [18:110]

He to whom the dominion over the heavens and the earth belongs, and who begets no offspring and has no partner in His dominion: for it is He who created everything and determined its nature in accordance with (His own) design. [25:2]

... should anyone who has done wrong and then has replaced the wrong with good: for, verily, I am All-Forgiving, Merciful! [27:11]

And thus whenever a warner comes to them...(the message) will only increase them in turning away. And they are proud on earth ... [35:42]

And the earth will shine bright with her Lord's light. And the record (of everyone's deeds) will be laid bare, and all the prophets will be brought forward, and all (other) witnesses; and judgment will be passed on them all with truth. And they will not be wronged. [39:69]

Whoever does what is just and right, does so for his own good; and whoever does evil, does so to his own detriment; and Allah never does the least wrong to His creatures. [41:46]

Certainly, everything have We created in measure and proportion. [54:49]

And provides for him in a manner beyond all expectation; and for everyone who places his trust in Allah, He (alone) is enough. Surely, Allah always attains His purpose: indeed, for everything has Allah appointed its (term and) measure. [65:3]

Thus have We determined (the nature of man's creation): and excellent indeed is Our power to determine (what is to be)! [77:23]

Who determines the nature (of all that exists), and then guides it (towards its fulfilment). [87:3]

## 4.14 The Complete Person

Yes, indeed: everyone who surrenders his whole being to Allah, and is a doer of good, shall have his reward with his Lord; and need have no fear, and neither shall they grieve. [2:112]

Granting wisdom to whom He wills: and whoever is granted wisdom has indeed been granted abundant wealth. But none bears this in mind save those who are endowed with insight. [2:269]

You cannot attain righteousness unless you spend on others out of what you love; and whatever you spend - verily, Allah has full knowledge of it. [3:92]

Say: "There is no comparison between the bad things and the good things, even though very many of the bad things may please you greatly. Be, then, conscious of Allah, O you who are endowed with insight, so that you might attain to a successful state!" [5:100]

For (even) before your time, (O Muhammad,) We never sent (as Our apostles) any but (mortal) men, whom We inspired – "If you do not know this, ask the followers of earlier revelation." [21:7]

O men! If you are in doubt as to the (truth of) resurrection, (remember that,) verily, We have created (every one of) you out of dust, then out of a drop of sperm, then out of a germ-cell, then out of an embryonic lump complete (in itself) and yet incomplete, so that We might make (your origin) clear to you ... [22:5]

If you are ungrateful - certainly, Allah has no need of you; none the less, He does not approve of ingratitude in His servants: whereas, if you show gratitude, He approves it in you. And no carrier of burdens shall be made to bear another's burden. In time, to your Lord you all will return, He will then tell you what you were doing, certainly, He has full knowledge of what is in the hearts (of men). [39:7]

The Bedouin say, "We believe." Say (O Muhammad): "You have not (yet) attained to faith; you should (rather) say, 'We have (outwardly) surrendered' - for (true) faith has not yet entered your hearts. But if you (truly) pay heed to Allah and His Apostle, He will not let the least of your deeds go to waste: for, certainly, Allah is All-forgiving, Merciful." [49:14]

In this, behold, there is indeed a reminder for everyone whose heart is wide-awake - that is, (everyone who) hears witnessing. [50:37]

Is it not time that the hearts of all who believe should feel humble at the remembrance of Allah and of the truth that has been revealed to them, lest they become like those who were granted revelation before, their hearts have hardened in time and many of them are (now) depraved. [57:16]

No, but they do not (believe in and, hence, do not) fear the life to come. [74:53]

And raised you high in fame . [94:4]

## 4.15 Full Consciousness

And do not marry an idolatress unless she believes: for a believing maid is better than an idolatress, even though she pleases you greatly. And do not give your women in marriage to an idolater unless they believe: for a believing slave is better than an idolater, even though he pleases you greatly. (Such as) these invite to the fire, whereas Allah invites to paradise, and to (the achievement of) forgiveness by His leave; and He makes clear His messages to mankind, so that they might bear them in mind. [2:221]

And undeviating is your Lord's way ... [6:126]

Said He: "Down with you, enemies to one another, having on earth your home and sustenance for a while. [7:24]

And We dispersed them as (separate) communities all over the earth; some of them were righteous, and some of them less than that. And We tried them (the latter) with blessings as well as with afflictions, so that they might mend their ways. [7:168]

Certainly, they who are guard (against evil) whenever any dark suggestion from Satan touches them, remember Allah and lo! they begin to see (things) clearly. [7:201]

This is a message to all mankind. Let them be warned by it, and let them know that He is the One and Only deity; and let those who are endowed with insight take this to heart! [14:52]

There are signs for those who reflect in the variety of colours created on earth. [16:13]

We explained in this book which We have revealed to you, (O Muhammad,) so that men may reflect on its messages, and that those who are endowed with insight may take them to heart. [38:29]

Or do you think of yourself equal to one who devoutly worships (Allah) throughout the night, prostrating himself or standing (in prayer), ever-mindful of the life to come, and hoping for his Lord's mercy? [39:9]

Blessed is He who ... has created seven heavens in harmony with one another: no fault will you see in the creation of the Most Gracious. And turn your vision once more: can you see any flaw? ... Yes, turn your vision again and yet again: your vision will return, dazzled and defeated. [67:1, 3-4]

# Chapter 5
# Earthly Life and the Hereafter

## 5.1 Transient Living

... who believe in that which has been revealed to you, (O Prophet,) as well as in that which was revealed before your time, it is they who in their innermost are certain of the life to come! [2:4]

And indeed, Allah made good His promise to you when, by His leave, you were about to destroy your enemies - until the moment when you lost heart and acted contrary to the (Prophet's) command, and disobeyed after He had brought you within view of victory for which you were longing. There were among you who cared for this world (alone), just as there were among you who cared for the hereafter: so in order to test you, He prevented you from victory. But now He has removed your sin: for Allah is limitless in His bounty to the believers. [3:152]

Say: "Brief is the enjoyment of this world, whereas the life to come is the best for all who are conscious of Allah - since none of you shall be wronged by as much as a hair's breadth (minutest). [4:77]

"To You, we have turned to in repentance!" (Allah) answered: "With My punishment I afflict whom I will - but My mercy embraces everything: and so I shall confer it on those who are conscious of Me and spend in charity, and who believe in Our messages. [7:156]

(Say to them) "You are like those who lived before your time. They were superior in power and wealth than you, and in children; and they enjoyed their share. And you have been enjoying your share - just as those who preceded you enjoyed their share; and you have been indulging in idle talk - just as they indulged in it. Their works did not benefit them in this world and the hereafter – those are the losers!" [9:69]

For them there is the good news (of happiness) in the life of this world and in the hereafter; nothing could ever alter Allah's promises, this is the supreme achievement. [10:64]

(They would know that) the life of this world is nothing but a passing delight and an amusement - whereas, the life in the hereafter is indeed the only life: if they only knew this! [29:64]

O humankind – you have, certainly been striving towards your Lord in hard striving - then you will meet Him! [84:6]

Return to thy Lord, well-pleased (and) pleasing (Him). [89:28]

For, certainly to your Lord all must return. [96:8]

## 5.2 Forms and Meanings

And We made the House, a place of pilgrimage to which people might come (again and again,) and a sanctuary: take then, the place whereon Abraham once stood as your place of prayer." [2:125]

Yea, indeed, We have created you, and then formed you; and then We said unto the angels, "Prostrate yourselves before Adam!" - whereupon they [all] prostrated themselves, save Iblis: he was not among those who prostrated themselves. [7:11]

And [as for thee], O Adam, dwell you and your wife in this garden, and eat, both of you, whatever you may wish; but do not approach this one tree, lest you become evildoers! [7:19]

And [thus] did We inspire Moses and his brother: "Set aside for your people some houses in the city, and [tell them], 'Turn your houses into places of worship, and be constant in prayer!' ... [10:87]

The Parable of those who take [beings or forces] other than God for their protectors is that of the spider which makes for itself a house: for, the frailest of all houses is the spider's house! Could they but understand this! [29:41]

And besides those two will be yet two [other] gardens–which, then, of your Lord's signs do you deny? – two [gardens] of the deepest green. [55:62-64]

... but Allah came to them whence they did not expect, and cast terror into their hearts; they demolished their houses with their own hands and the hands of the believers; therefore take a lesson, O you who have eyes! [59:2]

## 5.3 Veils and Deceptions

They try to deceive Allah and those who believe - while they deceive none but themselves, and do not perceive it. [2:9]

Certainly, the hypocrites seek to deceive Allah - while it is He who causes them to be deceived (by themselves). And when they rise to pray, they rise lazily only to be seen and praised by others, remembering Allah but seldom. [4:142]

And those who disbelieve were plotting against you, in order to restrain you, or to kill you, or to drive you out: they devised a plan; and Allah devised a plan – and Allah is the best of all planners. [8:30]

And should they seek to deceive you - Certainly, Allah is enough for you! He it is who has strengthened you with His favour, and with the believers. [8:62]

But as for those who disbelieve, their (good) deeds are like a mirage in the desert, which the thirsty assumes to be water - until, when he approaches it, he finds that it was nothing: instead, he finds (that) Allah (has always been present) with him, and (that) He will pay him his account in full - for Allah is swift in reckoning! [24:39]

Now certainly it is We who have created man, and We know what his innermost self whispers within him: for We are closer to him than his jugular-vein. [50:16]

"Indeed, you have been unmindful of this (Day of Judgment); but now We have lifted from you your veil, and your sight is sharp today!" [50:22]

Consider the passage of time! Verily, man is at a loss. [103:1-2]

## 5.4 Elusive Security

"And remember how He made you heirs to (the tribe of) 'Ad and established you on earth, so that you (are able to) build for yourselves castles on its plains and carve your homes out of mountains; remember, then, Allah's blessings, and do not act wickedly on earth by spreading corruption." [7:74]

Those who believe, and whose hearts find their rest in the remembrance of Allah - for, certainly, in the remembrance of Allah do hearts find their rest. [13:28]

"If only you had said, when you entered your garden, 'Whatever

Allah wills will come to pass, there is no power except Allah!' Even though you see me as having less wealth and offspring than you, it may be that my Lord will give me better than your garden - He may destroy your garden, into heap of barren dust. [18:39-40]

But Satan whispered to him, saying: "O Adam! Shall I lead you to the tree of eternal life; and a kingdom that will never decay?" [20:120]

He it is who turned them out of their homes, at the first gathering (for war), those from earlier revelation who disbelieved ... [59:2]

And provides for him in a manner beyond all expectation; and for everyone who places his trust in Allah He (alone) is enough. Certainly, Allah always attains to His purpose: (and) indeed, for everything has Allah appointed a (term and) measure. [65:3]

On that Day will man exclaim "Where do we escape to?" [75:10]

On a Day when everyone will (want to) run from his brother. [80:34]

Consider the passage of time, certainly, man is at a loss. [103:1-2]

## 5.5 Faithless Worldliness

They will ask you about fighting in the sacred month. Say: "Fighting in it is a grave offence; but turning men away from the path of Allah and denying Him, and (turning them away from) the Sacred Mosque and expelling its people from it - is more offensive in the sight of Allah, since persecution is worse that slaughter." (Your enemies) will not stop fighting against you until they have turned you away from your faith, if they can. But if any of you should turn away from his faith and die as a unbeliever - their works will not avail them in this world and the hereafter, destined for the fire, therein to abide. [2:217]

And as for those who disbelieve, I shall cause them to suffer severely in this world and in the hereafter, and they shall have none to help them. [3:56]

And leave those who have made amusement and fleeting pleasures their way of life and who are deceived by the life of this world, but remind them that in the life to come every human being shall be held accountable for whatever wrong he has done, and shall have none to protect him from Allah, and none to intercede for him; even though he may offer any conceivable ransom, it will not be accepted. It is these that will be held accountable for the wrong they have done; for them there is (in the life to come) a drink of burning despair, and grievous suffering awaits them because of their persistent refusal to acknowledge the truth. [6:70]

Say to them: "You are like those who lived before your time. They were superior in power and wealth than you, and in children; and they enjoyed their share. And you have been enjoying your share - just as those who preceded you enjoyed their share; and you have been indulging in idle talk - just as they indulged in it. Their works did not benefit them in this world and the hereafter – these are the losers!" [9:69]

Certainly, as for those who do not believe that they are destined to meet Us but content with the life of this world and do not look beyond it, and are heedless of Our messages – [10:7]

All this, because they hold this world's life in greater esteem than the life to come, and because Allah does not bestow His guidance upon people who disbelieve. [16:107]

We have readied grievous suffering for those who will not believe in the hereafter. [17:10]

And preferred the life of this world. [79:38]

## 5.6 Faith and Righteousness

Allah granted them the rewards of this world, as well as the choicest rewards of the life to come; for Allah loves those who do good. [3:148]

Surely, as for those who believe and do good - their Lord guides them aright by means of their faith. In the hereafter running waters will flow at their feet in gardens of bliss; and in that (state of happiness) they will call out, "You are limitless in your glory, O Allah!" - and will be answered with the greeting, "Peace !"And their call will close with (the words), "All praise is due to Allah, the Lord of all the worlds!" [10:9-10]

Allah grants abundant sustenance, for whom He wills or reduces it for whom He wills, and they (who are given abundance) rejoice in the life of this world - even though, as compared with the life to come, the life of this world is but a fleeting pleasure. [13:26]

But as for those who care for the (good of the) life to come, and strive for it as it ought to be striven for, and are (true) believers - they are the ones whose striving finds favour with Allah! [17:19]

And contain yourself in patience by the side of those who morning and evening invoke their Lord, seeking His countenance, and do not overlook them in a quest of the beauties of this world's life; and pay no attention to any whose heart We have rendered heedless of all remembrance of Us because he had always followed (only) his own desires, abandoning all that is good and true. [18:28]

Seek instead, by means of what Allah has granted you, (the good of) the life to come, without forgetting, your own (rightful) share in this world; and do good to others as Allah has done good to you; and do not seek to spread corruption on earth: for, certainly, Allah does not love those who spread corruption!" [28:77]

Therefore, (O believer,) endure all adversity with graceful patience. [70:5]

And endure with patience whatever people may say (against you), and avoid them with grace. [73:10]

But no, (O men,) you prefer the life of this world, although the life to come is better and more enduring. [87:16-17]

## 5.7 Perfections of Afflictions

Wherever you may be, death will overtake you - even though you be in towers raised high. Yet, when a good thing happens to them, some (people) say, "This is from Allah," whereas when evil falls on them, they say, "This is from you (O fellowman)!" Say: "All is from Allah." What, then, is wrong with these people that they cannot understand the truth of what they are told? [4:78]

Hence, do not spread corruption on earth after it has been well ordered. And call unto Him with fear and longing: verily, Allah's mercy is ever near the doers of good! [7:56]

Allah grants abundant sustenance, for whom He wills or reduces it for whom He wills, and they (who are given abundance) rejoice in the life of this world - even though, as compared with the life to come, the life of this world is but a fleeting pleasure. [13:26]

Observe how We bestow more sustenance on some over others:

but (remember that) the life to come will be far higher in degree and far greater in merit and sustenance. [17:21]

Your Lord knows you best, He will have mercy on you if He pleases or He will chastise you if He pleases and He has not sent you to be in charge of them. [17:54]

And (remember) whatever you are given (now) is but amusement in this world, and for its embellishment - whereas that which is with Allah is better and more enduring. Will you not, then, use your reason? [28:60]

Your worldly goods and your children are but a trial and a temptation, whereas with Allah there is a tremendous reward. [64:15]

Surely, it is We who have created man out of a drop of sperm intermingled, so that We might try him; and therefore We made him a being endowed with hearing and sight. [76:2]

O man - you have, certainly been striving towards your Lord in hard striving - then you will meet Him! [84:6]

Surely with every hardship comes ease, surely with every hardship comes ease. [94:5-6]

## 5.8 For Others' Sake?

And if a woman has reason to fear ill-treatment from her husband, or that he might turn away from her, it shall not be wrong for the two to set things right peacefully between themselves: for peace is best, and selfishness is ever-present in human souls. But if you do good and are conscious of Him - certainly, Allah is aware of all that you do. [4:128]

(As for) those who attain to faith and do good deeds - We do not burden any human being with more than he can bear - they are destined for paradise, therein to reside. [7:42]

Certainly, those who attain to faith and do good deeds and humble themselves before their Lord - they are destined for paradise, and there shall they reside. [11:23]

Corruption (and evil) has appeared on land and in the sea as an outcome of what men have earned, and so He will let them taste (the evil of) some of their doings, so that they might return (to the right path). [30:41]

Whoever does what is just and right, does so for his own good; and whoever does evil, does so to his self: and never does your Lord the least wrong to His creatures. [41:46]

For, (in the life to come,) all shall have their reward in accordance with whatever (good or evil) they did; He will repay them in full for their actions, and none shall be wronged. [46:19]

No sustenance do I ever demand of them, nor do I demand that they feed Me. [51:57]

And who give food for the love of Him - (however great be their own want of it) - to the needy, orphan, and the captive. [76:8]

## 5.9 Cleverness and Wisdom

Granting wisdom to whom He wills: and whoever is granted wisdom has indeed been granted abundant wealth. But none bears this in mind except those who are endowed with insight. [2:269]

... And Allah has revealed to you the book and the wisdom and He has taught you what you did not know and Allah's grace on you is immense. [4:113]

Behold, the hypocrites want to deceive Allah - while it is He who causes them to deceive themselves. And when they rise to pray, they rise lazily, only to be seen and praised by men, remembering Allah very seldom. [4:142]

To the people who (in the past) had been deemed weak (and were exploited), We gave as their heritage the eastern and western parts of the land that We had blessed. Your Lord's promise to the children of Israel was fulfilled in result of their patience in adversity; whereas We destroyed all that Pharaoh and his people had earned, and all that they had built. [7:137]

Those who had been weak (and got exploited) will say to those who had boasted in their arrogance: "No, what kept us away was your devising of false arguments, night and day, against Allah's messages, when you persuaded us to blaspheme against Allah and to claim that there are powers that could rival Him ..." [34:33]

Say (O Muhammad): "Behold, I am commanded to worship Allah, sincere in my faith in Him alone." [39:11]

And lo! They (unbelievers) will contend with each other in the fire (of the hereafter); and then the weak will say to those who had boasted in their arrogance, "Surely, we followed you, then, relieve us of some (of our) share of this fire?" [40:47]

He it is who has created the heavens and the earth in six periods, and established Himself on the throne (in power) ... [57:4]

Even though he may cover himself with excuses. [75:15]

## 5.10 War and Peace

O you who believe! Surrender yourselves wholly to Allah, and follow not Satan's footsteps, for, verily, he is your open enemy. [2:208]

Verily, they who believe, and emigrate (to escape persecution) striving hard in Allah's cause - it is they who may look forward to Allah's mercy: for Allah is All-Forgiving, Merciful. [2:218]

It is a just recompense for those who make war on Allah and His apostle, and endeavour to spread corruption on earth, that they are being slain ... and in the life to come more suffering awaits them. [5:33]

And so he led them on with deluding thoughts. But as soon as the two had tasted (the fruit) of the tree, they became conscious of their nakedness; and they began to cover themselves with leaves from the garden. And their Lord called to them: "Did I not forbid that tree to you and tell you, 'Certainly, Satan is your open enemy'?" [7:22]

They would argue with you about the truth after it had become manifest - just as if they were being driven towards death and witnessed it with their very eyes. [8:6]

O you who believe! Respond to the call of Allah and the Apostle whenever he calls you to that which will give you life; and know that Allah intervenes between man and his heart, and that to Him you shall be gathered. [8:24]

And Allah invites to the abode of peace, and guides him that wills to a straight way. [10:25]

Therefore, do not obey (the likes and dislikes of) those who deny the truth, but strive hard against them, (by means of this book), with utmost striving. [25:52]

When you meet in battle those who disbelieve, strike their necks until you overcome them fully, and then make them prisoners their bonds; but thereafter (set them free,) either by an act of grace or against ransom, so that the burden of war may be lifted; thus (shall it be). And had Allah willed, He could indeed punish them; but (He wills you to struggle) so as to test you by means of one another. And as for those who are slain in Allah's cause, never will He let their deeds go to waste. [47:4]

You are to believe in Allah and His Apostle, and to strive hard in Allah's cause with your possessions and your lives: this is for your own good - if you but knew it! [61:11]

(On the Day of Judgment,) every human being will be held to account for whatever he has earned. [74:38]

## 5.11 Durable Justice

And so We have willed you to be a community of the middle way, so that you might bear witness to the truth before all mankind, and that the Apostle might bear witness to you. We have appointed the direction of prayer which you have observed to make a clear distinction between those who follow the Apostle and those who turn back on their heels; this was indeed a hard test for all except those whom Allah has guided. Allah will surely not lose sight of your faith - certainly, Allah is All-Compassionate towards man, Merciful. [2:143]

For, certainly, those who have attained to faith in this book as well as those who follow the Jewish faith, the Sabians, and

Christians - all who believe in Allah and the Last Day and do good – shall have no fear and neither shall they grieve. [5:69]

For, truly and justly has your Lord's promise been fulfilled. There is no power that could alter His promises; and He alone is All-Hearing, All-Knowing. [6:115]

Certainly, Allah enjoins justice, and the doing of good, and generosity towards kinfolks; He forbids all evil deeds, shameful acts and oppression; He admonishes you (repeatedly) so that you might be mindful. [16:90]

Every human being is bound to taste death; and We test you through the bad and the good by way of trial: and to Us you must return. [21:35]

(And) he prayed: "O my Lord! Verily, I have sinned against myself! Grant me, then, your forgiveness!" And He forgave him - for, surely, He alone is Forgiving, Merciful. [28:16]

Be grateful to Allah, and whoever is grateful he is only grateful for his own self and whoever is ungrateful then surely Allah is Self Sufficient, Praised...Do not associate others with Allah: for, certainly, such (a false) association is indeed a grave sin! [31:12-13]

Say: "I believe in what Allah has revealed to me; and I am commanded to act justly between you. Allah is our Lord as well as your Lord. We are accountable for our deeds, and you are for your deeds. Let there be no contention between us and you: Allah will bring us all together - for to Him is all journeys' end." [42:15]

## 5.12 Failure, Success and Victory

"No strength have we today against Goliath and his forces!" those who knew with certainty that they were destined to meet Allah, replied: "How often has a small army overcome a larger one by Allah's leave! For Allah is with those who are patient in adversity." [2:249]

And hold fast, all together, to the bond with Allah, and do not draw apart from one another. And remember the blessings which Allah has bestowed upon you: how, when you were enemies, He brought your hearts together, so that through His blessing you became brothers; and when you were on the brink of a fiery abyss He saved you from it. In this way Allah makes clear His messages to you, so that you might find guidance. [3:103]

If Allah helps you, none can ever overcome you; but if He should forsake you, who could help you thereafter? In Allah, then, let the believers place their trust! [3:160]

And the Egyptian who bought him said to his wife "Make his stay honourable. Maybe he will be useful to us, or we may adopt him as a son." And so We established Joseph in the land and taught him the interpretation of events (dreams). And Allah has full control over his affair, most people know not. [12:21]

Surely, We have laid open before you a clear victory.' [48:1]

He called out to his Lord , "I am defeated, help me!" [54:10]

Whatever (spoils taken) from the people of those villages Allah has turned over to His Apostle, all of it belongs to Allah and the Apostle, and the family (of deceased believers), orphans, the needy, and the traveller, so that it may not be taken by turns among the rich. Accept (willingly) whatever the Apostle gives you, and refrain from (demanding) anything that he withholds from you; and remain conscious of Allah: for, certainly, Allah is severe in retribution. [59:7]

When Allah's help comes, and victory. [110:1]

## 5.13 Hell and Paradise

And do not marry an idolatress unless she believes: for a believing maid is better than an idolatress, even though she pleases you greatly. And do not give your women in marriage to an idolater unless they believe: for a believing slave is better than an idolater, even though he pleases you greatly. (Such as) these invite to the fire, whereas Allah invites to paradise, and to (the achievement of) forgiveness by His leave; and He makes clear His messages to mankind, so that they might bear them in mind. [2:221]

And (as for you), O Adam, reside you and your wife in this garden, and eat, both of you, whatever you may wish; but do not approach this one tree, lest you become an evildoer. [7:19]

He alone grants life and death; and to Him you must return. [10:56]

For, (on that Day,) paradise will be brought within sight of the God conscious. [26:90]

... warn (them) of the Day of the Gathering, which is beyond all doubt: (the Day when) some shall find themselves in paradise, and some in the blazing flame. [42:7]

(And) they add, "That, would be a return with loss!" [79:12]

The day on which man will recollect what he strove after and Hell shall be made manifest to him who sees, then as for him who is inordinate and prefers the life of this world then surely Hell is the abode. And as for him who fears to stand in the presence of his Lord and forbids the soul of its low desires then surely the garden that is the abode. [79:35-41]

He who (in the life to come) shall have to endure the great fire ... [87:12]

Who whispers in the hearts of men. [114:5]

**5.14 Wholesome Life**

Who believe in the unseen, and are constant in prayer, and spend on others out of what We provide for them as sustenance. [2:3]

Those to whom We have given the book and who follow it as it ought to be followed it is they who (truly) believe in it; whereas all who choose to deny its truth - it is they, they who are the losers! [2:121]

It is lawful for you to have intercourse with your wives during the night preceding the fast: they are as a garment for you, and you are as a garment for them... He has removed this hardship from you... and eat and drink until you can discern the white streak of dawn against the blackness of night, and then resume fasting until nightfall; These are the bounds set by Allah: do not, then transgress. Thus Allah makes clear His messages to mankind, so that they might remain conscious of Him. [2:187]

Will you blaspheme against Him who has created you out of dust, and then out of a drop of sperm, and in the end has fashioned you into a (complete) man? [18:37]

Have they not travelled through the earth, allowing their hearts to gain wisdom, and allowing their ears to hear? Yet, verily, it is not the eyes that have become blind - but the hearts that are in their breasts! [22:46]

The trustworthy spirit (Gabriel) has brought it from on high. [26:193]

Limitless in His glory is He who has created pairs in whatever the earth produces, and in themselves, and in that of which they have no knowledge. [36:36]

O you believe! Remain conscious of Allah, and believe in His Apostle, (and) He will double his mercy, and will grant you a light with which you shall walk, and will forgive you; for Allah is All-Forgiving, Merciful. [57:28]

But as for man, whenever his Lord tries him by His generosity and by letting him enjoy a life of ease, he says, "My Lord has been generous towards me." [89:15]

## 5.15 Death and the Hereafter

Every human being is bound to taste death: but only on the Day of Resurrection will you be repaid in full (for whatever you have done) - he that shall be drawn away from the fire and brought into paradise will indeed have gained a triumph: for the life of this world is nothing but an enjoyment of deception. [3:185]

And on that Day We shall (call all mankind and) leave them to surge like waves against one another; and the trumpet (of judgment) will be blown, and We will gather them all together. [18:99]

Say: "Which is better - that, or the paradise of eternal life which has been promised to the God conscious as their reward and their journey's end. [25:15]

(For Him,) your creation and resurrection is like (the creation and resurrection of) a single soul: for, certainly, Allah is All-Hearing, All-Seeing. [31:28]

And (then) the trumpet (of resurrection) will be blown - and lo! out of their graves will they all rush towards their Lord! [36:51]

And (on that Day,) the trumpet (of judgment) will be sounded, and all that are in the heavens and earth will swoon away, except those whom Allah wills. And then it will sound again - and standing (before the Seat of Judgment), they will begin to see (the truth)! [39:68]

And (in the end) the trumpet (of resurrection) will be blown: that will be the Day of a warning fulfilled. [50:20]

All that lives on earth or in the heavens is bound to pass away; but your Lord's Face will abide eternally, full of Majesty and Glory. [55:26-27]

The Day when the trumpet (of resurrection) is sounded and you all come forward in multitudes. [78:18]

For, certainly, to your Lord all must return. [96:8]

## 5.16 Universal Resurrection

Who, when calamity befalls them, say, "Verily, to Allah do we belong and, certainly to Him we shall return." [2:156]

And He it is who has brought you (all) into being out of one living entity, and (has appointed for each of you) a time-limit (on earth) and a resting place; clearly, We have spelled out these messages to people who can grasp the truth! [6:98]

Their Lord gives them the glad tiding of the mercy (that flows) from Him, and of (His) acceptance, and of the gardens which await them, full of lasting bliss. [9:21]

Surely, as for those who believe and do good - their Lord guides them aright by means of their faith. (In the life to come,) running waters will flow at their feet in gardens of bliss. [10:9]

And every human being's destiny have We tied to his neck; and on the Day of Resurrection We shall bring out for him a (personal) record which he will find wide open. [17:13]

On that Day, all dominion shall belong to Allah. He shall judge between them: so, all who had believed and did good shall find themselves in gardens of bliss. [22:56]

And He is the One who gives me to eat and to drink. [26:79]

Some faces will on that Day be bright with happiness. [75:22]

So when the stars are made to lose their light and when the heaven is rent asunder and when the mountains are carried away as dust and when the apostles are gathered at their appointed time, from what day has the term been fixed? [77:8-12].

And (partake of) whatever fruit they may desire. [77:42]

## 5.17 Perfection of Destiny

But there are among them such to say, "O our Lord ! Grant us good in this world and good in the life to come, and keep us safe from suffering through the fire." [2:201]

And indeed, Allah made good His promise to you when, by His leave, you were about to destroy your enemies - until the moment when you lost heart and acted contrary to the (Prophet's) command, and disobeyed after He had brought you within view of victory for which you were longing. There were among you who cared for this world (alone), just as there were among you who cared for the hereafter: so in order to test you, He prevented you from victory. But now He has removed your sin: for Allah is limitless in His bounty to the believers. [3:152]

O you who believe! What is wrong with you that, when you are called upon, "Go to war in Allah's cause," you cling heavily to the earth (reluctant)? Would you content yourselves with (the comforts of) this worldly life in preference to (the good of) the life to come? [9:38]

If you do not go to war (in Allah's cause), He will chastise you with grievous chastisement, and will place another people in your stead - whereas you shall in no way harm Him: for, Allah has the power to will anything. [9:39]

Who turn away from the path of Allah and desire to make it crooked and they are disbelievers in the hereafter ... Truly it is they, they who in the life to come shall be the losers! [11:19-22]

But as for those who refused to acknowledge the truth and reject Our messages -and to the announcement of a life to come - they will be brought forth to suffering. [30:16]

"O my people! This worldly life is but a brief enjoyment, whereas, certainly, the life to come is the home abiding." [40:39]

O you who believe! Do not befriend people whom Allah has condemned! They (who would befriend them) are indeed bereft of all hope of a life to come - just as the unbelievers are bereft of all hope of those who are in their graves. [60:13]

# Chapter 6
# Prophets of Islam

## 6.1 Many Prophets with One Message

Behold, the only (true) religion in the sight of Allah is (man's) self-surrender to Him; and those who were given revelation before took, out of mutual jealousy, to different views (on this point) only after knowledge of it had come to them. [3:19]

And Muhammad is only an apostle; all the (other) apostles have passed away before him: if, he dies or is slain, will you turn about on your heels? [3:144]

"And, O our Lord, grant us that which you have promised us through your apostles, and do not disgrace us on Resurrection Day! Verily, You never fail to fulfil Your promise." [3:194]

And we inspired other apostles whom we have mentioned to you as well as apostles we have not mentioned to you; and to Moses Allah addressed his word; (We sent all these) apostles as messengers of good news and as warners, so that men might have no excuse before Allah after (the coming of) these apostles . [4:164-165]

And, indeed, We sent Our messages to people before your time, and afflicted them with misfortune and hardship so that they might humble themselves. [6:42]

But We send (Our) messengers as heralds of good news and as warners ... [18:56]

So has Allah, the Almighty, the Wise, revealed to you and to those who preceded you; ...to Him belongs all that is in the heavens and all that is on earth; and He is Most Exalted, Tremendous. [42:3-4]

## 6.2 Different Cultures and People

Say: "O followers of the book (earlier revelation)! Come to that which you and we hold in common; that we shall worship none but Allah, and that we shall not ascribe divinity to other than Him, and that we shall not take human beings for our Lords except Allah," And if they turn away, then say: "Bear witness that it is we who have surrendered ourselves to Him." [3:64]

O you who have attained to faith! Pay heed to Allah, and pay heed to the Apostle and to those from among you who have been entrusted with authority (who have knowledge and cautious awareness); and if you are at disagreement over any matter, refer it to Allah and the Apostle ... [4:59]

And, indeed, there came to them Our apostles with all evidence of the truth: yet, certainly, notwithstanding all this, many of them go on committing all manner of unrestrained behaviour on earth. [5:32]

And, indeed, We sent (Our messages) to people before your time, (O Prophet,) and afflicted them with misfortune and hardship so that they might humble themselves. [6:42]

Indeed, there has come to you (O mankind) an Apostle from among yourselves: the thought that you might suffer in the hereafter weighs heavily on him; he is full of concern for you and full of compassion and mercy towards the believers. [9:128]

And never have We sent any apostle with a message unless it be in his own people's tongue, so that he might make (the truth) clear to them. [14:4]

Whoever chooses to follow the right path follows it for his own good; and whoever goes astray does so to his own hurt; and no bearer of burdens shall be made to bear another's burden. Moreover, We would never chastise (any community for the wrong they may do) until We have sent an apostle (to them). [17:15]

And (every time) We send to them an apostle from among themselves, (he told them:) "Worship Allah (alone): you have no deity other than Him. Will you not, then, become conscious of Him?" [23:32]

And how many a prophet did We send to people of past times! [43:6]

## 6.3 Prophetic Qualities

Even as We have sent to you an apostle from among yourselves to convey Our messages, and to cause you to grow in purity, and to impart to you revelation and wisdom, and to teach you that which you know not. [2:151]

For, when they come to hear (understand) what has been revealed to the Apostle, you can see their eyes overflow with tears, because they recognize its truth; (and) they say: "O our Lord! We do believe; recognise us as one who bears witness to the truth. [5:83]

"Do not grieve, certainly, Allah is with us." [9:40]

Yet they say: "What sort of apostle is this (man) who eats food (like all other mortals) and goes about in the market-places? Why has not an angel been sent down to him, to act as a warner together with him?" [25:7]

He replied: "No indeed! My Lord is with me, (and) He will guide me!" We then inspired Moses, "Strike the sea with your staff!" - Then it parted, and each part appeared like a huge mountain. [26:62-63]

Muhammad is not the father of any one of your men, but is Allah's Apostle and the Seal of all Prophets. [33:40]

Remain, then, patient in adversity, just as all of the apostles, endowed with firmness of heart, bore themselves with patience. [46:35]

... to convey to them His messages, and to cause them to grow in purity, and to impart to them the book as well as wisdom. [62:2]

Or is it that (they fear) your asking them for a reward, (O Prophet,) so that they would be burdened with debt (if they listened to thee)? [68:46]

And did not feel any urge to feed the needy. [69:34]

But he would not attempt the ascent (an obstacle). And what could make you conceive what the ascent is. (It is) the freeing of a neck (to set a slave free) or to feed on the day of hunger, an orphan near of kin, or a needy lying in the dust (poor wretch in misery). [90:11-16]

Have you ever considered him who rejects all moral law? Certainly, it is this (kind of man) that pushes the orphan away, and does not urge to feed the needy. [107:1-3]

## 6.4 Courage and Sacrifice of Prophets

We have not made you their keeper, and neither are you responsible for their conduct. [6:107]

If you do not help the Apostle, then (know that Allah will do so - just as) Allah helped him at the time when those who disbelieve drove him away, (and he was but) one of two: when these two were (hiding) in the cave, (and) the Apostle said to his companion, "Grieve not, certainly, Allah is with us." And Allah sent His tranquillity on him. [9:40]

Oh, certainly, they who are close to Allah - have no fear and neither do they grieve. [10:62]

And (so it is) We have not taught him (the Prophet) poetry, nor would it have suited this (message): it is but a clear reminder, showing the truth. [36:69]

Remain patient in adversity, just as all of the apostles, endowed with firmness of heart, bore themselves with patience. And do not ask for a speedy fate of the unbelievers ... [46:35]

Consider the pen, and all that they write with it! You are not, by your Lord's grace, insane! Certainly, yours will be a reward never-ending for, behold, you indeed keep to a sublime way of life; and (one day) you will see, and they (who now scorn you) will see, which of you is afflicted with madness. Certainly, your Lord is fully aware as to who has strayed from His path, Just as He is fully aware of those who have found the right way. So, do not condone the unbelievers; they would like you to be lenient with them, so that they might be (easy) with you. [68:1-9]

Certainly, this (Qur'an) is indeed the (inspired) word of a noble apostle, and however little you may (be prepared to) believe it, is not the word of a poet; or a soothsayer ... Now if he whom We entrust with it had dared to attribute some (of his own) sayings to Us, We would indeed have seized him by his right hand, and would indeed have cut his life-vein (aorta). And none of you could have saved him! [69:40-47]

## 6.5 Living Islam

And if My servants ask you about Me - certainly, I am near; I respond to the call of him who calls, whenever he calls to Me: let them, then, respond to Me, and believe in Me, so that they might follow the right way. [2:186]

Certainly, the only (true) religion in the sight of Allah is Islam (man's self-surrender to Him); and those who were given revelation before, took out of mutual jealousy, to differing views, only after knowledge had come to them. But as for the disbelievers in the truth of Allah's messages - certainly, Allah is swift in reckoning! [3:19]

Behold, We have revealed to you this sacred book, making clear the truth, so that you may judge between people in accordance with what Allah has taught you. So, do not contend with those who are not true to their trust. [4:105]

And who could be of better faith than he who surrenders his whole being to Allah and does good, and follows the creed of Abraham, who turned away from all that is false - seeing that Allah exalted Abraham with His love? [4:125]

Forbidden to you is carrion, blood, the flesh of swine, that over which any name other than Allah's has been invoked, the animal that has been strangled, or beaten to death, or killed by a fall, or gored to death, or savaged by a beast of prey, save that which you (yourselves) may have slaughtered while it was still alive; and forbidden to you is all that has been slaughtered on idolatrous altars. You are forbidden to seek through divination what the future may hold in store for you: this is sinful conduct. Today, those who disbelieve have despaired of your religion: do not fear them, but stand in awe of Me! Today have I perfected your way of life, and have completed My favour to you, and chosen for you Islam (self-surrender) as your way of life.' However as for him, who is driven (to what is forbidden) by dire necessity (severe hunger) and not by an inclination to transgress - certainly, Allah is All-Forgiving, Merciful. [5:3]

And (know) that this leads straight to Me: follow it, then, and do not follow other ways, lest they cause you to deviate from His way. (All) this has He enjoined on you, so that you might remain conscious of Him. [6:153]

And Moses said: "O my people! If you believe in Allah, place your trust in Him - if you have surrendered yourselves to Him!" [10:84]

And strive hard in Allah's cause with all the striving that is due to Him. So, be constant in prayer, and pay the purifying dues, and hold fast to Allah ... [22:78]

But your Lord says: "Call Me, (and) I shall respond to you!" [40:60]

"Since all evidence of the truth has come to me from my, Lord I am forbidden to worship (any of) those beings whom you invoke instead of Allah; and I am commanded to surrender myself to the Lord of all the worlds." [40:66]

But good and evil cannot be equal, repel evil with something that is better – and he who had enmity (may then become) as though he had (always) been close (to you), a true friend! [41:34]

Steadfastly uphold the faith, and do not break up your unity therein. And even though that to which you call them appears oppressive to those who disbelieve, Allah draws to Himself anyone who is willing, and guides to Himself anyone who turns to Him. [42:13]

## 6.6 Equity, Charity & Justice

The pilgrimage will take place in the months appointed for it. And whoever undertakes the pilgrimage in those (months) will, abstain from sexual intercourse, from all wicked conduct, and from quarrelling; and whatever good you may do, Allah is aware of it. And make provision for yourselves - but, certainly, the best of all provisions is God consciousness: remain, then, conscious of Me, O you who are endowed with insight! [2:197]

... Allah wants to lighten your burdens: for man has been created weak. [4:28]

O you who believe, do not devour your property among yourselves unjustly except that it be trading by your mutual consent, and do not kill yourselves, surely Allah is merciful to you. [4:29]

... the people who had been deemed weak, We gave as their heritage the eastern and western parts of the land that We had blessed. And your Lord's promise to the children of Israel was fulfilled in result of their patience in adversity; and We destroyed all that Pharaoh and his people had earned, and all that they had built. [7:137]

Those who keep up prayer and spend generously out of what we have given them. [8:3]

(And We said:) "If you persevere in doing good, you will be doing good to yourselves; and if you do evil, it will be against yourselves." [17:7]

And give due to the close relative, as well as to the needy and the traveller, but do not waste senselessly. [17:26]

My righteous servants shall inherit the earth. [21:105]

But it was Our will to bestow Our favour on you who were deemed weak in the land, and to make them leaders and to make them heirs. [28:5]

O men! It is you who stand in need of Allah, whereas He alone is self-sufficient, the One to whom all praise is due. [35:15]

And who give food - (however great be their own want of it) - to the needy, the orphan, and the captive, (saying, in their hearts,) "We feed you for the sake of Allah alone: we do not desire reward nor thanks from you." [76:8-9]

**6.7 Laws and Boundaries**

He has forbidden to you only carrion, and blood, and the flesh of swine, and that over which any name other than Allah's has been invoked; but if one is driven by necessity - neither coveting it nor exceeding his immediate need - no sin shall be on him: for, behold, Allah is All-forgiving, Merciful. [2:173]

And do not consume each other's possessions wrongfully, and neither seek access to the rulers with a view to devouring sinfully, and knowingly, anything that by right belongs to others. [2:188]

It is lawful for you to have intercourse with your wives during the night preceding the (day's) fast ... and eat and drink until you can discern the white streak of dawn against the blackness of night, and then resume fasting until nightfall; these are the bounds set by Allah: do not, then transgress. [2:187]

... you enjoin the doing of what is right and forbid the doing of what is wrong ... [3:110]

Judge, then, between the followers of earlier revelation in accordance with what Allah has revealed ... to every one of you have We appointed a (different) law and way of life. [5:48]

And, finally, (O Muhammad,) We have set you on a way by which the purpose (of faith) may be fulfilled, so follow this (way), and follow not the likes and dislikes of those who do not know (the truth). Certainly, they could never be of any help to you ... [45:18-19]

O prophet! When you (intend to) divorce women, divorce them with a view to the waiting period appointed for them, and count the period (carefully), and be conscious of Allah, your Lord. Do not expel them from their homes; and neither shall they (be made to) leave unless they become openly guilty of immoral conduct. These, then, are the bounds set by Allah - and he who transgresses the bounds set by Allah does indeed sin against himself: you know it not, after that Allah may well cause something new to come about. [65:1]

... indeed, to everything has Allah appointed its (term and) measure. [65:3]

## 6.8 Religious Rituals and Practices

O mankind! Worship your Lord, who has created you and those who lived before you, so that you might remain conscious of Him. [2:21]

And seek assistance in steadfast patience and prayer: and this, indeed, is a hard thing for all but the humble in spirit. [2:45]

These are the bounds set by Allah: do not, then transgress. Thus, Allah makes clear His messages to mankind, so that they might remain conscious of Him. [2:187]

And who could be of better faith than he who surrenders his whole being to Allah and does good, and follows the creed of Abraham, who turned away from all that is false - seeing that Allah exalted Abraham with His love? [4:125]

This is (to be borne in mind). And anyone who honours the symbols set up by Allah (shall know that,) surely, these (symbols derive their value from) the piety of hearts. [22:32]

Convey whatever of this book has been revealed to you, and be constant in prayer: for, certainly, prayer restrains (one) from despicable actions and from all that which is despicable; and remembrance of Allah is indeed the greatest (good). And Allah knows all that you do. [29:45]

Now, when man is distressed, he calls out to his Lord, turning to Him; but as soon as He gives him relief by His Grace, he forgets Him whom he invoked before, and claims that there are other powers that could rival Allah. [39:8]

Those who sustain the throne (high ranking angels) and those around him celebrate the praise of their Lord and believe in Him and ask protection for those who believe ... [40:7]

Certainly, Allah is my Lord as well as your Lord; so worship (none but) Him: this (alone) is a straight way! [43:64]

But prostrate yourselves before Allah, and worship (Him alone)! [53:62]

Let them, therefore, worship the Lord of this house ... [106:3]

## 6.9 Relationships, Duties and Courtesies

And so, when you divorce women and they are about to reach the end of their waiting-term, then either retain them in a fair manner or let them go in a fair manner. But do not retain them against their will in order to hurt (them): for he who does so sins indeed against himself. And do not take (these) messages of Allah in a frivolous spirit; and remember the blessings with which Allah has graced you, and all the revelation and the wisdom which He has bestowed on you from on high in order to remind you; and remain conscious of Allah, and know that Allah has full knowledge of everything. [2:231]

You will incur no sin if you divorce women while you have not yet touched them or appointed anything to them; but (even in such a case) make provision for them - the affluent according to his means, and the poor according to his means - a provision in a equitable manner: this is a duty upon all who would do good. [2:236]

There is no compulsion in religion. Truly the right way has become distinct from error. ... Allah is near those who have faith, taking them out of darkness into the light – whereas near those who disbelieve are powers of evil that take them out of the light into darkness; it is they who are destined for the fire, therein to reside. [2:256-257]

Because of this did We decree, on the children of Israel that if anyone kills a human being unless it be (in punishment) for murder or for spreading corruption on earth - it shall be as though he had murdered all mankind; whereas, if anyone saves a life, it shall be as though he had saved the lives of all mankind. [5:32]

Whoever shall come (before Allah) with a good deed will gain ten times the like thereof; but whoever shall come with an evil deed will be punished with no more than the like thereof; and none shall be wronged. [6:160]

And whenever they spend anything (for the sake of Allah), be it little or much, and whenever they move on earth (in Allah's cause) - it is recorded in their favour, and Allah will grant them the best reward for all that they have been doing. [9:121]

And never have We sent any apostle except with a message in his own people's tongue, so that he might make (the truth) clear to them; but Allah lets go astray him that wills (to go astray), and guides him that wills (to be guided) - for He alone is Almighty, Wise. [14:4]

For your Lord has commanded that you will worship none but Him. And do good to your parents. Should one of them, or both, attain to old age in your care, never say "Ugh" to them or scold them, but (always) speak to them with respectful speech, and spread over them humbly the wings of your tenderness, and say: "O my Lord! Grant your mercy to them, as they cherished and reared me when I was a child!" [17:23-24]

No bearer of burdens shall be made to bear another's burden. [53:38]

It is they who say "Do not spend anything on those who are with Allah's Apostle, so that they (may be forced to) leave." However, to Allah belong the treasures of the heavens and the earth: but this truth the hypocrites cannot grasp. [63:7]

## 6.10 Perfect Worship

Allah - there is no deity except Him, the Ever-Living, Lord of all that exists. Neither slumber nor sleep overtakes Him. To Him belongs all that is in the heavens and all that is on earth. Who is there that could intercede with Him, unless it be by His leave? He knows what happens to them in this world and in the hereafter, whereas they cannot attain to His knowledge except that which He wills. His power encompasses the heavens and the earth, and their preservation does not weary Him. Moreover, he alone is Exalted, Tremendous. [2:255]

We have never sent any apostle except that he should be obeyed by Allah's leave. If, then, after having sinned against themselves, they would but come to you and ask Allah to forgive them - with the Apostle, too, praying that they be forgiven - they would surely find that Allah is an acceptor of repentance, Merciful. But no, by your Lord, they do not believe until they make you an arbitrator between them and then do not find any resistance in their hearts as to what you have decided and submit completely. [4:64-65]

O you who believe! Hold fast to your belief in Allah and His messenger, and in the book which He has revealed to His messenger, as well as in the revelation which He sent down before ... [4:136]

Behold, Allah has bought from the believers their lives and their possessions, promising them paradise in return, (and so) they fight in Allah's cause, and slay, and are slain ... [9:111]

For whoever is blind (of heart) in this (world) will be blind in the life to come, and still further astray from the way. [17:72]

Blessed is He who has revealed to His servant the standard by which to discern the true from the false, so that it might be a warning to the world. [25:1]

We have revealed to you a book in Arabic in order that you may warn the foremost of all cities and all who live around it - warn of the Day of Gathering, which is beyond any doubt: some shall find themselves in paradise, and some in the blazing flame. [42:7]

(Be patient:) for this is nothing else but a reminder (from Allah) to all mankind. [68:52]

Consider the daybreak; and the ten nights! [89:1-2]

O you who believe! Respond to the call of Allah and the Apostle whenever he calls you to that which will give you life; and know that Allah intervenes between man and his heart, and that to Him you shall be gathered. [8:24]

## 6.11 The Way of Muhammad

And Mohammed is only an apostle; all the (other) apostles have passed away before him: if, then, he dies or is slain, will you turn back on your heels? [3.144]

Say (O Prophet): "I do not say to you, 'Allah's treasures are with me,'; nor do I know the unseen'; nor do I say to you, 'I am an angel': I only follow what is revealed to me. [6.50]
And thus it is that against every prophet We have set up as enemies the evil forces from among humans as well as from among jinn who whisper to one another glittering half-truths meant to delude the mind ... [6.112]

Say (O Prophet): "It is not within my power to bring benefit or avert harm from myself, except as Allah may please. And if I knew the unseen (that which is beyond the reach of human perception), abundant good fortune - would surely be mine, and no evil would ever touch me. I am nothing but a warner, and a herald of good news to people who will believe." [7:188]

Indeed, there has come to you an Apostle from among yourselves: grievous to him is your falling into distress; he is full of concern for you and full of compassion and mercy towards the believers. [9:128]

And We have sent you as (an evidence of Our) mercy towards all the worlds. [21:107]

Say: "It has been revealed to me that your deity is only one deity (Only Allah): will you, then, surrender yourselves to Him?" [21:108]

Muhammad is not the father of any one of your men, but is Allah's Apostle and the Seal of all Prophets. And Allah has indeed full knowledge of everything. [33.40]

O Prophet - surely, We have sent you as a witness, and as a herald of good news and a warner. And as one inviting to Allah by his permission and as a light giving torch (guidance and knowledge). [33.45-46]

To this end, then, summon (all mankind), and pursue the right course, as you have been commanded; and do not follow their likes and dislikes, but say: "I believe in what has been revealed by Allah ; and I am commanded to bring about justice between you. Allah is our Lord as well as your Lord. To us shall be accounted our deeds, and to you, your deeds. Let there be no contention between us and you: Allah will bring us all together - for with Him is all journeys' end." [42.15]

Say (O Prophet): "No reward do I ask of you for this other than (that you should) love and show kindness to your near relatives."For, if anyone gains (the merit of) a good deed, We shall grant him through it an increase of good ..." [42.23]

Mohammed is Allah's Apostle; and those who are with him are firm and unyielding towards all who disbelieve, (yet) full of mercy towards each other. You can see them bowing down, prostrating themselves, seeking favour with Allah and (His) acceptance: their marks are on their faces, traced by prostration ... [48.29]

And surely you have sublime morals. [68.4]

## 6.12 Humanity and Divinity

Theirs shall be a home of peace with their Lord; and He shall be their guardian in result of what they have been doing. [6:127]

O children of Adam! Do not allow Satan to seduce you in the same way as he caused your ancestors (Adam and his wife) to be driven out of the garden: he deprived them of their garment (of God consciousness) in order to make them aware of their nakedness ... [7:27]

Behold, Allah has bought of the believers their lives and their possessions, promising them paradise in return ... Rejoice, then, in the pledge which you have made with Him: for this, is the supreme achievement. [9:111]

Oh, surely, they who are close to Allah – have no fear, and neither will they grieve. [10:62]

And before you, We did not send any messengers but (mortal men,) who indeed ate food (like other human beings) and went about in the marketplaces: for (it is like that). We cause you to be a means of testing one another. Are you able to endure with patience? For your Lord is All-Seeing! [25:20]

True servants of the Most Gracious are (only) they who walk with humility on earth, and who, whenever the foolish address them, reply with (words of) peace. [25:63]

He it is who bestows His blessings upon you, with His angels (echoing Him), so that He takes you out of the depths of darkness into the light. And, indeed, He is Merciful to the believers. [33:43]

Verily, Allah and His angels salute the Prophet: O you who believe, salute him and give yourselves up (to his guidance) in total self-surrender! [33:56]

A book, the messages have been clearly spelled out in Arabic for people of (innate) knowledge. [41:3]

(He has sent) an apostle who conveys to you Allah's clear messages, so that He might remove those who believe and do good deeds out of the depths of darkness into the light. And whoever believes in Allah and does what is right and just, him will He admit into gardens through which running waters flow, therein to reside eternally: indeed, Allah will grant him the best provision! [65:11]

Those who are constant in their prayer. [70:23]

## 6.13 Universal Mercy and Grace

And obey Allah and the Apostle, so that you might be graced with mercy. [3:132]

Say "Peace be upon you, Your Lord has willed the law mercy on Himself - so that if any of you does a bad deed out of ignorance, and thereafter repents and lives correctly, He is All-Forgiving, Merciful." [6:54]

And call on Him with cautious awareness and hope: surely, Allah's mercy is ever near those who do good! [7:56]

Why, do think it is strange that news from your Lord should have come to you through a man from among yourselves, so that he might warn you, and that you might become conscious of Allah, and that you might be graced with His mercy? [7:63]

My mercy embraces all things: and so I shall confer it on those who are conscious of Me and spend in charity, and who believe in Our signs. [7:156]

Allah has promised the believing men and woman gardens beneath which rivers flow to reside in them and excellent dwellings in gardens of Eden and best of all is Allah's excellent pleasure, that is the grand achievement. [9:72]

And yet, I am not trying to absolve myself: for, surely, man's inner self does incite (him) to evil, and only they are saved on whom my Lord bestows His mercy. Certainly, my Lord is All-Forgiving, Merciful!" [12:53]

And (O Prophet,) We have sent you as (an evidence of Our) mercy to all the worlds. [21:107]

And even were We to show them mercy and remove whatever distress afflicting them, they would still persist in their arrogance, blindly stumbling to and fro. [23:75]

Say "O you servants of Mine who have transgressed against your own selves! Despair not of Allah's mercy. Certainly, Allah forgives all sins - for, certainly, He alone is All-Forgiving, Merciful!" [39:53]

Now as for those who believe and did good deeds, their Lord will admit them to His mercy: that, will be (their) manifest achievement! [45:30]

For, certainly, all who say, "Our Lord is Allah", and thereafter stand firm (in their faith) – will have no fear, and neither shall they grieve. [46:13]

# Chapter 7
# Salvation and Enlightenment

## 7.1 Information and Transformation

Allah is the protector of those who believe, taking them out of darkness into the light – those who disbelieve have false gods as protectors that take them out of the light into darkness: it is they who are destined for the fire, to reside therein. [2:257]

But abstain from sinning, be it open or secret - for, those who commit sins shall be rewarded for all that they have earned. [6:120]

He (everyone) has hosts of angels (helpers) in succession - that protect him by command of Allah. Certainly, Allah will not change the (good and natural) condition of people as long as they do not alter it by themselves ... [13:11]

Just as you cannot lead the blind (of heart) out of their error; nor can you make to hear except those who believe in Our messages, and surrender themselves to Us. [27:81]

Do men think that on their (mere) saying, "We believe", they will be left to themselves, and will not be tested? [29:2]

As for those who strive hard in Our cause - We shall most certainly guide them to paths that lead to Us: for, certainly, Allah is with the those who do good. [29:69]

They know only the outer appearance of this world's life, whereas of the hereafter they are heedless. [30:7]

Are you not aware that Allah has made subservient to you all that is in the heavens and all that is on earth, and has lavished upon you His blessings, both outward and inward? And yet, among men there is many a one that argues about Allah without having any knowledge (of Him), without any guidance, and without any light-giving revelation. [31:20]

The living and the dead are not equal. Certainly, Allah can make to hear whomever He wills, whereas you cannot make to hear those that are (dead of heart like the dead) in their graves: [35:22]

Can you, perhaps, make the deaf to hear, or show the right way to the blind or to such as are obviously lost in error? [43:40]

Consider the soul and Him who perfected it, and inspired it with consciousness of right and wrong, he is indeed successful who purified it and he is indeed a failure who corrupts it. [91:7-10]

## 7.2 Special Warnings

And, after all this, your hearts hardened and became like stones, or even harder; and surely there are stones from which streams gush forth; there are some from which, when split, water flows; and there are some that fall down due to awe of Allah. And Allah is not unmindful of what you do! [2:74],

Are you not aware of that (king) who argued with Abraham about his Lord, (simply) because Allah had granted him kingship? Lo! Abraham said: "My Lord is He who grants life and deals death." (The king) replied: "I (too) grant life and deal death!" Abraham said, "Surely, Allah causes the sun to rise in the east; can you, then, cause it to rise in the west!" Then he who disbelieved remained dumbfounded; Allah does not guide people who (deliberately) do wrong. [2:258]

Certainly, Allah does not forgive that anything should be associated with Him, although He forgives any lesser sin to whomever He wills: for he who associates others than Allah has indeed committed a grave sin. [4:48]

But all that has been bestowed on you by your Lord is bound to make many of them (the Jews) yet more stubborn in their arrogance and in their denial of the truth. And so We have cast enmity and hatred among them until Resurrection Day; every time they light the fires of war, Allah extinguishes them... [5:64]

O you who believe! Do not deprive yourselves of the good things of life which Allah has made lawful to you, but do not transgress the bounds of what is right: certainly, Allah does not love those who transgress the bounds of what is right. [5:87]

Thus, partake of the lawful, good things which Allah grants you as sustenance, and be conscious of Allah, in whom you believe. [5:88]

Thus it will be more likely that people will offer testimony in accordance with the truth - or else they will (have cause to) fear that their oaths will be refuted by the oaths of others. Be, then, conscious of Allah, and attentive to Him; for Allah does not bestow His guidance upon iniquitous people. [5:108]

O children of Adam! Beautify yourselves for every act of worship, and eat and drink (freely), but do not waste: verily, He does not love the wasteful! [7:31]

But as for those who are bent on denying Our messages - We shall bring them low, step by step, without their perceiving how it came about: [7:182]

And guard yourselves of that affliction which not only befalls on those who do wrong exclusively; and know that Allah is severe in retribution. [8:25]

If you have reason to fear treachery from people (with whom you have made an agreement), cast it back at them in a just manner: for, verily, Allah does not love the treacherous! [8:58]

No wrong did We do to them, but it was they who wronged themselves. And when your Lord's judgment came to pass, those deities of theirs which they invoke instead of Allah proved of no avail whatsoever to them, and brought them no more than utter perdition. [11:101]

## 7.3 Inner Integrity

For you take vengeance on us only because we have come to believe in our Lord's messages as soon as they came to us. "O our Lord: Shower us with patience in adversity, and make us die as men who have surrendered ourselves to you!" [7:126]

We have now come to you (with a message from) your Lord; and (know that His) peace shall be (only) on those who follow (His) guidance. [20:47]

Now they who disbelieve ask, "Why has not the Qur'an been revealed to him in one single revelation?"(It has been revealed) in this manner so that We might strengthen your heart by it - for We have revealed its parts gradually (that they form one consistent whole.) [25:32]

Only he (will be happy) who comes before Allah with a wholesome heart. [26:89]

Now whoever surrenders his whole being to Allah, and does good, has indeed taken hold of a support that never fails: for with Allah rests the final outcome of all events. [31:22]

Allah puts forth a parable: A man who has for his masters, several partners, (all of them) at variance with one another, and a man depending wholly on one person: can these two be deemed equal as regards their condition? (No,) all praise is due to Allah (alone): but most of them do not understand this. [39:29]

Invoke, then, Allah, sincere in your faith in Him alone, however hateful this may be to those who disbelieve! [40:14]

And whosoever's scale is light, they are those who lost themselves because they rejected Our signs. [7:9]

The (servant's) heart did not disbelieve what he saw. [53:11]

So that you may not despair over whatever (good) has escaped you nor exult (unduly) over whatever (good) has come to you: for, Allah does not love any of those who, out of self-conceit, act in a boastful manner. [57:23]

## 7.4 Living Faith

Allah is near those who believe, taking them out of darkness into the light – those who disbelieve have false gods as protectors that take them out of the light into darkness: it is they who are destined for the fire, to reside therein. [2:257]

And, lo, Abraham said: "O my Lord! Show me how you give life to the dead!" Said He: "Have you, then, no faith?" (Abraham) answered: "Yes, but (let me see it) so that my heart may be set fully at rest." [2:260]

"We believe in it; the whole (of the book) is from our Lord - none takes this to heart (in remembrance) except those who are endowed with insight. [3:7]

... all who believe in Allah and the Last Day and do good deeds - no fear will they have, and neither shall they grieve. [5:69]

Judgment rests only with Allah. In Him, I have placed my trust. And all who have trust must place their trust in Him (alone). [12:67]

And Allah endows those who avail themselves of (His) guidance with an ever-deeper consciousness of the right way; and good deeds, the fruit of which endures forever, are, in your Lord's sight, of far greater merit (than any worldly goods), and yield far better returns. [19:76]

No community can ever hasten (the end of) its term - and neither can they delay it. [23:43]

And to convey this Qur'an (to the world). Whoever, therefore, chooses to follow the right path, follows it but for his own good; and if any wills to go astray, say (to him): "I am only a warner!" [27:92]

Certainly, you cannot guide whom you love: but it is Allah who guides whom He pleases; and He is fully aware of all who would let themselves be guided. [28:56]

He will guide them and will reset their minds to a (better state). And will make them enter the Garden that was already made known to them. [47:5-6]

And to everyone who is conscious of Allah, He (always) grants a way out (of unhappiness), and provides for him in a manner beyond all expectation; and for everyone who places his trust in Allah, He (alone) is enough. Verily, Allah always attains to His purpose: indeed, to everything has Allah appointed its (term and) measure. [65:2-3]

Say: "He is the Most Gracious: we believe in Him, and in Him have we placed our trust; and in time you will come to know which of us was lost in manifest error." [67:29]

## 7.5 Path of Relief and Gladness

Fighting is prescribed for you, even though it be hateful to you; it may well be that you hate a thing that is good for you, and love a thing that is bad for you: and Allah knows, whereas you do not know. [2:216]

Believers are only they whose hearts tremble with awe whenever Allah is mentioned, and whose faith is strengthened whenever His messages are conveyed to them; and who in their Lord place their trust – [8:2]

And they who believe, and migrated and are striving hard in Allah's cause, as well as those who shelter and help them - it is they who are truly believers! They shall be forgiven, and be given an honourable provision. [8:74]

Surely, those who believe and do good deeds and humble themselves before their Lord - they are destined for paradise, and there shall they reside. [11:23]

... those who believe, and whose hearts find their rest in the remembrance of Allah - Surely, in the remembrance of Allah hearts do find rest. [13:28]

Truly, the believers shall attain to a happy state: those who humble themselves in their prayer, and who turn away from all that is frivolous, and who are intent on inner purity; and who are mindful of their chastity, (not giving way to their desires) except with their spouses – or those whom they rightfully possess for then, behold, they are free of all blame, whereas such as seek to go beyond that limit are truly transgressors; and who are faithful to their trusts and to their pledges, and who guard their prayers. It is they, who shall inherit paradise; therein shall they reside. [23:1-11]

But as for those who strive hard in Our cause - We shall certainly guide them onto paths that lead to Us: for, surely, Allah is indeed with the doers of good. [29:69]

"O my people! Yours is the authority today, (and) most eminent are you on earth: but who will rescue us from Allah's punishment, once it befalls us?" Said Pharaoh: "I only show you that which I see myself; and I would never make you follow any path but the right way!" [40:29]

Tell all who believe that they should forgive those who do not believe...It is for Him (alone) to reward people for whatever they may have earned. [45:14]

... and to everyone who is conscious of Allah, He (always) grants a way out. [65:2]

## 7.6 Path of Despair and Sadness

But when they are told, "Follow what Allah has revealed," some answer, "No, we shall follow (only) that which we found our forefathers believing in and doing." Why, even if their forefathers did not use their reason at all, and were devoid of all guidance? [2:170]

"But do not believe anyone who does not follow your own faith." Say: "Surely, all (true) guidance is Allah's guidance." Say: "All Grace is in Allah's hands and He bestows it upon whom He wills." [3:73]

Yet when misfortune decreed by Us befell them, they did not humble themselves, but rather their hearts grew hard, for Satan had made all their doings seem good to them. [6:43]

If you do not go to war (in Allah's cause), He will chastise you with grievous chastisement, and will place another people in your stead - whereas you will do Him no harm. For, Allah has the power to will anything. [9:39]

Surely, as for those who will not believe in Allah's messages, Allah does not guide them; and grievous suffering will be their lot. [16:104]

To him who cares for (no more than the enjoyment of) this fleeting life We readily hasten to him what We please, but in the end We deliver him to (the suffering of) hell; which he will have to endure disgraced and disowned! [17:18]

As for those who will not believe in the hereafter, We have made their actions appear good to them, and so they stumble blindly to and fro. [27:4]

But when Our clear signs came to them, they said, "This is clearly spellbinding deception!" [27:13]

Certainly We did test those before them; most certainly will Allah mark out those who prove themselves true, and most certainly will He mark out those who are lying. [29:3]

And then leave them alone, and wait, for they too, are waiting ... [32:30]

Have you ever considered he who makes his desires his god, and whom Allah has let go astray, knowing (that his mind is closed to all guidance), and whose hearing and heart He has sealed, and upon whose sight He has placed a veil? Who, then, could guide him after Allah (has abandoned him)? Will you not then be mindful? [45:23]

No, but man is evidence against himself, though he presents his excuses. [75:14-15]

## 7.7 Anchored Transcendence

And thus have We willed you to be a community of the middle way (balanced and just) ... [2:143]

They rejoice in the glad tiding of Allah's blessings and bounty, and (in the promise) that Allah will not fail to reward the believers. [3:171]

"Behold, people have gathered against you; so beware of them!" This only increased their faith, so they answered, "Allah is enough for us; and how excellent a guardian is He!" [3:173]

For all shall attain degrees according to their (conscious) deeds - and your Lord is not unaware of what they do. [6:132]

To him who cares for (no more than the enjoyment of) this fleeting life We readily hasten to him what We please ... But as for those who care for the life to come, and strive for it as it ought to be striven for, and are (true) believers - they are the ones whose striving finds favour with Allah! [17: 18-19]

Behold how We bestow (on earth) more bounty on some of them than on others: but (remember that) the hereafter will be far higher in degrees and far greater in merit and bounty. [17:21]

And never say about anything, "Verily, I shall do this tomorrow," without (adding), "if Allah wills." And if you should forget (at the time, and become aware of it later), call your Lord to mind and say: "I pray that my Lord may guide me, and bring me even closer than this, to (a consciousness of) what is right!" [18:23-4]

The metaphor of those who take (beings or forces) other than Allah for their protectors is like that of the spider which makes for itself a house: surely, the frailest of all houses is the spider's house. Could they but understand this! [29:41]

Say: "Allah is enough for me! On Him do the reliant place their trust." [39:38]

As for those who say, "Our Lord is Allah," and then steadfastly pursue the right way - on them do angels descend, (saying) "Fear not and grieve not, but receive good news of the garden which has been promised to you!" [41:30]

"O human soul that has attained complete peace! Return to your Lord, well-pleased (and) pleasing (Him): [89:27-28]

## 7.8 Happy Sobriety

The way of those on whom you have bestowed your blessings, not of those who have been condemned, nor of those who go astray! [1:7]

Rejoicing in that (martyrdom) which Allah has bestowed on them out of His bounty. And they rejoice for the sake of those who have been left behind and have not yet joined them, that they will have no fear, and neither will they grieve. [3:170]

Upon him who shall be spared on that Day, He will indeed have bestowed His mercy: and this will be a manifest achievement. [6:16]

A book which We have revealed to you so that you might bring forth mankind, by their Lord's permission, out of the depths of darkness into the light: to the way that leads to the Almighty, the One to whom all praise is due. [14:1]

And indeed, We have set up in the heavens great constellations, and endowed them with beauty for all to behold. [15:16]

Surely, you shall have no power over My servants – except those who are (already) lost in error and follow you. [15:42]

Certainly, those who are conscious of Allah shall find themselves in the midst of gardens and springs. [15:45]

Within a few years - with Allah is the power of decision, before and after. And on that day will the believers (too, have cause to) rejoice. [30:4]

So that Allah might forgive your faults, past as well as future, and give you the full measure of His blessings, and guide you on a straight way. [48:2]

And (then,) the twilight of death brings with it the truth - that (very thing, O man,) from which you would always look away (trying to escape)! [50:19]

Which, then, of your Lord's blessings can you deny? He has given freedom to the two seas, so that they meet. [55:18-19]

As for those who in their Lord's Presence stand in awe, two gardens of paradise are made ready. [55:46]

## 7.9 Beyond Ease and Difficulty

And if My servants ask you about Me - certainly, I am near; I respond to the call of him who calls, whenever he calls to Me; let them, then, respond to Me, and believe in Me, so that they might follow the right way. [2:186]

Are these people waiting, perchance, for Allah to reveal Himself to them in the shadows of the clouds, together with the angels - although (by then) all will have been decided, and to Allah all things will have been brought back? [2:210]

And remember your Lord unceasingly, and glorify His limitless glory by night and by day. [3:41]

When two groups from among you were about to lose heart, although Allah was near them; it is in Allah that the believers must place their trust. [3:122]

And compete with one another to attain to your Lord's forgiveness and to a paradise as vast as the heavens and the earth, which has been prepared for the God conscious. [3:133]

Those who have been warned by other people, "Behold, people have gathered against you; so beware of them!" This only increased their faith, so that they answered, "Allah is enough for us; and how excellent a guardian is He!" [3:173]

It was to them that We entrusted revelation, wisdom.... And now, although the unbelievers may choose to deny these truths, (know that) We have entrusted them to people who will never deny them . [6:89]

We would be guilty of blaspheming against Allah, were we to return to your ways after Allah has saved us from them! It is not conceivable that we should return to them - unless Allah, our Lord, so wills. Our Lord embraces all things within His knowledge; in Allah do we place our trust. O our Lord! Lay open the truth between us and our people - for you are the best of all to lay open the truth! [7:89]

Know that Allah is sublimely exalted. The Ultimate Sovereign, the Ultimate Truth: and do not approach the Qur'an in haste, until it has been revealed to you in full, but say: "O my Lord, increase me in knowledge!" [20:114]

Every human being is bound to taste death; and We test you (all) through the bad and the good (things of life) by way of trial: and to Us you all will return. [21:35]

And as for those who believe and do good, We shall certainly remove their bad deeds, and shall certainly reward them in accordance with the best that they ever did. [29:7]

And place your trust in Allah (alone): for none is as worthy of trust as Allah. [33:3]

But Allah will safeguard all who were conscious of Him, (and will grant them happiness) by virtue of their (inner) triumphs; no evil will ever touch them, and neither will they grieve. [39:61]

But (since) good and evil cannot be equal, repel evil with

something that is better - and lo! he between whom and yourself was enmity (may then become) as though he had (always) been close to you, a true friend! [41:34]

Now as for those who take others beside Him for their protectors - Allah watches them, and you are not responsible for their conduct. [42:6]

And (remember that) whatever you are given (now) is but for the (passing) enjoyment of life in this world - whereas that which is with Allah is far better and more enduring. It will be given to all who believe and place their trust in their Lord. [42:36]

Certainly, the suffering decreed by your Lord will indeed come to pass. [52:7]

O you who believe! Turn to Allah in sincere repentance: it may well be that your Lord will remove from you your bad deeds, and will admit you into gardens beneath which running waters flow, on a Day which Allah will not shame the Prophet and those who believe with him: their light will gleam before them and on their right; they will pray: "O our Lord! Perfect our light, and forgive us our sins: for, surely, you have the power to will anything!" [66:8]

Surely, they think it to be something far away. [70:6]

## 7.10 God Consciousness

And if you doubt any part of what We have, revealed upon Our servant then produce a chapter of similar merit, and call upon any other than Allah to bear witness for you - if what you say is true! [2:23]

So remember Me, and I shall remember you; and be grateful to Me, and do not deny Me. [2:152]

... when misfortune befalls them, say, "Surely, to Allah do we belong and, surely, to Him we shall return." [2:156]

Surely, the only (true) religion in the sight of Allah is Islam (self-surrender to Him) ... [3:19]

And think of your Lord humbly and with awe, and without raising your voice, in the morning and evening; and do not allow yourself to be heedless. [7:205]

Believers are they whose hearts tremble with awe whenever Allah is mentioned, and whose faith is strengthened whenever His messages are conveyed to them; and who place their trust in their Lord. [8:2]

As for anyone - be it male or female - who does good and believes – those shall We certainly cause to live a good life and surely We shall grant them their reward in accordance with the best that they ever did. [16:97]

And had We not made you firm (in faith), you might have inclined to them a little. [17:74]

Continue to remind, for, surely, the remembrance will profit the believers. [51:55]

Whoever is willing may remember Him. [80:12]

Surely to your Lord all must return. [96:8]

## 7.11 Unitive Resonance

You have already had a sign in the two armies that met in battle, one army fighting in Allah's cause and the other denying Him; with their own eyes (the former) saw the others as twice their own number: Allah strengthens with His help whom He wills. In this, certainly, there is a lesson for all who have sight. [3:13]

Our Lord! We believe in what you have revealed, and we follow the messenger; include us then, with all who bear witness!" [3:53]

Say "I do not say to you, 'Allah's treasures are with me,' nor do I know the unseen; nor do I say to you, 'I am an angel': I but follow what is revealed to me. Say: "Can the blind and the seeing be equal? Will you not, then, reflect?" [6:50]

Clear evidence has come to you from your Lord. Whoever, therefore, chooses to see, does so for his own good; and whoever chooses to remain blind, does so to his own loss. "I am not your keeper." [6:104]

Yet if the people of those communities had believed and been conscious of Us, We would indeed have opened up for them blessings out of heaven and earth: but they disbelieved - and so We took them to task through what they (themselves) had been doing." [7:96]

And whenever your Lord brings forth offspring from the children of Adam, He calls on them to bear witness about themselves: "Am I not your Lord?" - to which they answer: "Yes, indeed, we do bear witness to it!" in case you say on the Day of Resurrection, "Surely, we were unaware of this" [7:172]

And yet, when you do not produce any miracle for them, some

say, "Why do you not seek to obtain it?" Say: "I only follow whatever is being revealed to me by my Lord: this (revelation) is clear proof from your Lord, and a guidance and mercy to people who will believe." [7:203]

And there are among them those who look towards you; but can you show the right way to the blind even though they cannot see? [10:43]

Have they not travelled through the earth, allowing their hearts to gain wisdom, and allowing their ears to hear? Certainly it is not the eyes that have become blind - but the hearts that are in their breasts! [22:46]

The blind and the seeing are not equal. [35:19]

And We have set a barrier before them and a barrier behind them, and We have enveloped them in veils so that they cannot see. [36:9]

This is a clear insight for mankind, and a guidance and mercy for people with certainty. [45:20]

And every soul shall come forward with its driver and a witness. [50:21]

Just as (there are signs) within your own selves: can you not, then, see? [51:21]

And We are closer to him than you, but you do not see. [56:85]

For, they who believe in Allah and His messengers - it is they who are, loyal, and the martyrs are with their Lord; they have their reward and their light. [57:19]

But no! I swear by that which you see, and that which you do not see. [69:38-39]

Yes indeed! His Lord did see all that was in him! [84:15]

Witnessed by all who have been drawn close to Allah. [83:21]

# BOOKS

O is a symbol of the world, of oneness and unity. In different cultures it also means the "eye," symbolizing knowledge and insight. We aim to publish books that are accessible, constructive and that challenge accepted opinion, both that of academia and the "moral majority."

Our books are available in all good English language bookstores worldwide. If you don't see the book on the shelves ask the bookstore to order it for you, quoting the ISBN number and title. Alternatively you can order online (all major online retail sites carry our titles) or contact the distributor in the relevant country, listed on the copyright page.

See our website www.o-books.net for a full list of over 500 titles, growing by 100 a year.

And tune in to myspiritradio.com for our book review radio show, hosted by June-Elleni Laine, where you can listen to the authors discussing their books.

mySpiritRadio